THE HISTORY OF

OPERA

FOR BEGINNERS

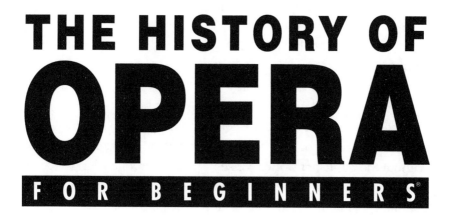

THE HISTORY OF
OPERA
FOR BEGINNERS

BY
RON DAVID

ILLUSTRATIONS BY
SARA WOOLLEY

FOR BEGINNERS®

For Beginners LLC
155 Main Street, Suite 211
Danbury, CT 06810 USA
www.forbeginnersbooks.com

A For Beginners® Documentary Comic Book
Copyright © 2013

Cataloging-in-Publication information is available from the Library of Congress.

ISBN # 978-1-934389-79-9 Trade

Manufactured in the United States of America

For Beginners® and Beginners Documentary Comic Books® are published by For Beginners LLC.

First Edition

10 9 8 7 6 5 4 3 2 1

contents

Dear reader: After careful consideration I have decided not to use the various dots, dashes and elegant accent marks of French, German, Italian, etc, beautiful though they are. In my opinion you can only make the reader feel all, *God, it's something else I don't know about.* To me that's exactly the kind of snobbery that turns people away from opera. This book on opera is written in plain unaccented English.

INTRODUCTION TO
OPERA FOR BEGINNERS

> If we resist our passions, it is more due to their weakness than our strength.　—La Rochefoucauld

> Intense feeling carries with it its own universe.　—Albert Camus

Or, to put that another way:

> "Too much of a good thing can be wonderful"　—Mae West

THE SHAWSHANK REDEMPTION

Q: What is the best way to introduce new people to opera?

A: There is a 3:49 segment in the movie *The Shawshank Redemption* that does a better job of introducing new people to opera than any book in the world, including mine. That scene has opened more people to the powerful emotional upside of opera than anything I know.

Q: How can I see it?

A: It's simple. Turn on your computer; go to **GOOGLE**; type in **"Wolfgang Amadeus Mozart – The Shawshank Redemption"**; select the **YouTube** option. Then watch and listen. It's only 3:49 long.

Q: Why do you think it's so powerful?

A: The first thing that comes to mind is the music: Mozart at his finest, sung with elegance (by Gundula Janowitz and Edith Mathes); but there have been other beautifully sung arias and duets from opera that didn't have anywhere the impact of *Shawshank*.

Q: Why do you think that happened?

A: I think that Morgan Freeman's monologue offered a sort of "template" or legitimization for how massively one can be moved by the music even if you don't understand a word of it! And how you may be neutering its beauty by trying too hard to understand it literally.

> *"I have no idea to this day what those two Italian ladies were singing about. Truth is, I don't want to know. Some things are best left unsaid. I'd like to think they were singing about something so beautiful, it can't be expressed in words, and makes your heart ache because of it. I tell you, those voices soared higher and farther than anybody in a gray place dares to dream. It was like some beautiful bird flapped into our drab little cage and made those walls dissolve away, and for the briefest of moments, every last man in Shawshank felt free."*

I think the movie gave people a taste, not only of the transcendent music, but of how opera's power could enter the souls of the most unlikely people imaginable. Is it realism? Of course not. Does it give you a sense of opera's potential to move you massively, no matter how hard-assed and tough you are? **YES, absolutely.**

MORE about how *The Shawshank Redemption* helps newcomers understand opera can be found in **Act 3** of this book **LISTENING to Opera: the Way It's Really Done.**

NOBODY LOVES THE FAT LADY

> **"This is my second opera. . . . Fat lady sang. Despised it!"**
> —Steward Copeland, drummer for The Police (the rock group)

Before we move on, let's deal with a few questions that hover in the air at the mere mention of opera.

Q: Why do so many of you smart suave sexy people hate opera?

A: Two reasons:

1) Because you think it's snobby, uptight, pretentious Museum Music.

2) Opera SINGERS. Most people don't know enough about opera to hate it. But you know in an instant when you hate a singer. You hate the Fat Lady. (For the purposes of this book, men with loud voices and Operatic Eyebrows fall under the general heading of the Fat Lady.)

Q: Why are most introductory books to opera useless?

A: Virtually every Intro to Opera I've come across seems to have been written by a clever guy, often in cahoots with a professional musician, both of whom who seem to have been born listening to opera.

If the absurdity of that doesn't strike you right off, imagine if (for example) you spoke only English and wanted to learn Spanish. Would you get a teacher who spoke only Spanish? Of course you wouldn't! You need a teacher who spoke both languages!

People who were born listening to opera have no idea what it's like to come to it from the outside. They don't speak our language—not in words, experience, or emotions. (My old semantics teacher would say that they have different "referents" than we do. The same words have such different meanings to us and them that we really are speaking different languages.)

Q: What is so good about my background?

A: The very commonness of it. In Detroit where I grew up there weren't a lot of opera houses. I was brought up on Little Richard, Bo Diddley, Elvis, the Drifters, Platters, Ella, Sinatra, Miles, Coltrane, Mahalia, Beatles, Stones, Aretha....in other words—**REAL Music!** Somewhere along the line I became an opera fanatic. I don't like opera, I *love* it. I know firsthand what it takes to make the transition from popular music to opera. That's why I'm the perfect person to introduce you to opera.

In the interest of getting on with it, I will give only brief answers to the following questions. More complete answers can be found in **Act 3**.

Q: Do I have go to an opera house and see a performance of an opera to learn about opera?

A: NO—you don't have to go to an Opera House to begin listening to opera. Every opera fan I know begins listening at home. I will describe the Do It Yourself approach to opera in the Appendix.

Q: Opera books are very specific about which operas to see but they don't seem to be the least bit fussy about the singers. Is that a realistic approach?

A: NO—no matter what most opera books or reviews say, **SINGERS are by far the most important variable in opera**. Every opera lover I know is incredibly fussy and specific about opera singers. Anyone who advises you to attend a performance without knowing the singers is essentially donating your money to an Opera House and wasting your time. How fussy are opera lovers about singers? Every major Opera House carries the stipulation that if a scheduled singer fails to show up for a performance, *your money will NOT be refunded*.

People travel all over the world to see certain singers. Imagine travelling halfway around the world to see Pavarotti or Domingo—and they don't show up!

Death is no excuse, Luciano!

WHAT EXACTLY IS OPERA?

> "Opera is music drama."
>
> —Richard Wagner (1813-83)

> "Opera is when a guy gets stabbed in the back and, instead of bleeding, he sings"
>
> —Ed Gardner (1905-63)

Actually, opera is two things: Technically, opera is a stage play, a drama—in which the characters sing all or most of the dialogue. A stage play set to music.

Unless you hate it.

When people say "I hate opera," they don't mean "I hate stage plays set to music"—the same people might tell you how much they liked *Phantom of the Opera* or *Porgy and Bess*. So when people say they hate opera, they generally mean, "I hate opera **SINGERS**."

So you don't hate OPERA. You hate...
(This isn't nit-picking, it's an important distinction!)
You hate... Opera SINGERS!

What can I tell you? In many cases, you're right. Some opera singers really stink. (Remind me to tell you why bad opera singing is a lot like bad s-e-x.)

The fact that opera is technically a stage play—a drama—set to music will almost certainly end up being irrelevant in determining whether you love it or hate it. The determining factors are the **singers** and the **songs**—the arias or operas.

You think you hate bad singers! La Scala opera house in Milan, Italy is famous for having the most knowledgeable and discriminating audience in opera...

One evening a tenor appearing at La Scala in Verdi's *Il Trovatore* sang the flashy aria "*Di quella pira*." When he finished, the audience requested an encore, so the proud tenor sang the aria again. When he finished the encore, the ornery La Scala fans demanded *another* encore! The tenor was feeling like the son of Caruso until one of the opera lovers spilled the beans:

There are few things as hideous as a bad opera singer. Stick around: I'll guide you around the bad ones and to the great ones.

(But opera seems so . . . intimidating!)

Let me give you some motherly advice: treat opera like a junkyard dog: if you're ever attacked by a rabid junkyard opera, don't run, don't move, above all don't show fear. Just lie there and relax. It's just music!

Let us start with the radical assumption that opera is just plain music. Not snob music. Not uppity music. Gettin' down music. Italian rock 'n roll, R&B, Gospel, let-it-all-hang-out music.

Italian SOUL music!

You probably think I'm making this up. HA!

ITALIAN SOUL

"It's difficult to talk about soul without being misunderstood. A singer can have expression of soul, yet sing off pitch and out of rhythm and do nothing with the words. Expression of soul goes beyond the words into the realm of ineffable emotions. It used to be known as 'il fuoco sacro'–'the sacred fire.' Before that it was called 'Il cantar che nell'anima si sente' 'singing that is sensed in soul.'"

"Expressive Singing" by Stephan Zucker
Opera Fanatic magazine [spring, 1986]

OPERA IS <u>LITERALLY</u> ITALIAN SOUL MUSIC!

It is no accident that African American singers are starring in opera houses all over the world. But I will save my aria about the similarity between Opera and Gospel singing until later. It's about time for the opera to hit the fan.

First, a word about the organization of this book.

OPERA FOR BEGINNERS is divided into <u>four</u> easy pieces:

1. Opera History & Composers
2. Opera Singers
3. Listening to Opera: (the Way It's REALLY Done)
4. The Most Listener-Friendly Operas and Their Stories

WHY?

- To give you a clear and simple overview of opera.
- For quick and easy referencing—find what you want instantly.
- To help you leap across entire chapters in a single bound if your soul gets pushy.

Reading about opera is like reading about puberty: the words go one way, the feeling goes another. If I were in your shoes (and I once was) I would consider reading **Act 3 (LISTENING to Opera)** <u>first</u>.

WARNING! Opera is a lot different than you think it is.

I'm out to get you, baby!

Everything about opera is different than you think it is. Including its history.

ACT ONE:
OPERA HISTORY & COMPOSERS

"I did **not** say history was bunk.
I said it was bunk **to** **me**. I
didn't need it very bad."

— Henry Ford

I suppose the point of that quote is we all "need it very bad" whether
we realize it or not?
(... on the other hand, you won't die without it.)

SCENE 1:
PRE-OPERATIC ROOTS AND EARLY HISTORY

OPERA'S ANCIENT ROOTS
(...or, Who Do We Blame?)

Opera's origins are usually traced back to the dramas of ancient Greece, and left at that. But that isn't playing fair with cultures that laid the groundwork and predated Greece by thousands of years. By the time Aeschylus wrote the first Greek "tragedy" (Drama), elegant folks in Mesopotamia, Africa and the Far East had been refining Music and Literature for 3000 years!

Here are a few highlights:

4000 BC–	Harps and flutes were being played in Egypt
3000 BC–	The Egyptians invent the Heb-Sed, Sumerians (Iraq) write the first epic tale: "Gilgamesh"
2500 BC–	Chinese develop a five tone musical scale; the first epic poetry is written in Babylon (Iraq)
2000 BC–	The first novel is written in Egypt: "The Story of Sinuhe"
1000 BC–	Professional musicians sing and play in ancient Israel
800 BC–	The earliest written music appears in Samaria (Ancient Palestine)
484 BC–	Aeschylus writes the first Greek tragedy

By the time Aeschylus wrote the first Greek drama Egyptians had been doing the **Heb-Sed** for over 2000 years!

"Skuza bro', but what is a "Heb-Sed?"

The Heb-Sed

In old, <u>old</u>, OLD Egypt, when the king got too rickety to rock 'n rule, they iced the old geezer! Around 3000 BC, the Egyptians, creative dudes that they were, decided to try replacing the <u>real</u> murder with a ritual "pretend" murder: the **Heb-Sed**.

The **Heb-Sed** evolved into Passion Plays in which the Egyptians acted out stories from Egypt's glorious past. Evidence suggests that the Passion Plays were often sung and accompanied by music.

Around 600 BC hundreds of Greek ships hit the sea to escape the grouchy Spartans. So many Greeks settled in Egypt that the Pharaoh gave them a city! The Greeks were impressed with Egyptian temples, Egyptian religion and they were truly dazzled by the Egyptian Passion Plays!

In 484 BC, **Aeschylus** wrote the first **Greek "tragedy."**

THE HEB-SED, the root of Greek tragedy, was created by Egyptians some 2500 years before the Greeks "invented" Drama. It is not a question of multiculturalism. It is a matter of simple intellectual honesty.

(So the Greeks invented Drama in approximately the same sense that Pat Boone invented "*Blueberry Hill*" - capish ?)

If you're looking for someone to blame for the origin of opera, blame the Egyptians, blame the Mesopotamians, blame the Chinese, blame the Greeks ... blame Human Nature. People everywhere have the impulse to sing and act out stories, so opera in some form seems to be hardwired into us.

Origin is one thing, perfection is another. The evolution of opera in the West has been dominated by the interplay—sometimes collision—of the Italian and German schools of opera.

But we are getting ahead of ourselves.

THE ANCIENT GREEKS
Aristotle

From what historians know of Greek tragedy, much of the play was chanted or sung. Although the music hasn't survived, Aristotle and his contemporaries tell us that music was an important part of Greek tragedy. From **Aristotle's** classical definition of tragedy:

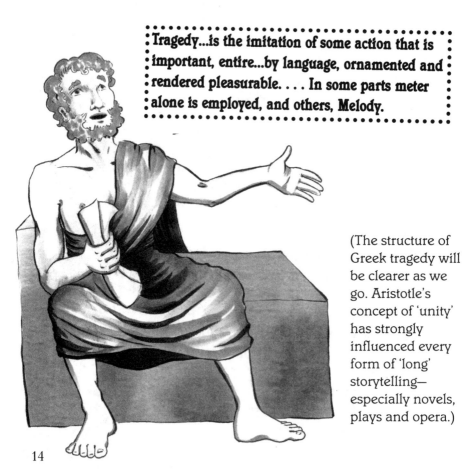

Tragedy...is the imitation of some action that is important, entire...by language, ornamented and rendered pleasurable. . . . In some parts meter alone is employed, and others, Melody.

(The structure of Greek tragedy will be clearer as we go. Aristotle's concept of 'unity' has strongly influenced every form of 'long' storytelling—especially novels, plays and opera.)

14

Music

The musical parts of Greek tragedy were never allowed to stand on their own or to compete with the text. Greek playwrights believed that the Music had to be kept within strict bounds or it would overpower the Drama.

It's not that the Greeks were afraid of music-they just understood its power.

Greek playwrights didn't mix comedy and tragedy. Greek comedy was spoken—although the chorus was sung. The chorus was often in the form of animals—flies, frogs or sheep—and their singing foolishly parodied the chanting tragic choruses.

THE ANCIENT ROMANS
A Funny Thing Happened...

Roman Dramas also used Music. Roman actors and actresses sometimes sang their lines, as did the choruses. The tragedies of **Seneca**—plays like **Medea**, **The Trojan Women**, and **Hercules on Oeta**—followed the Greek model and included a chorus to be sung.

Some historians consider Roman comedies the ancestors of our Broadway musicals.

The two most famous Roman comic playwrights, **Plautus** and **Terence**, used songs in their plays ...

> Stephen Sondheim's *A Funny Thing Happened on the Way to the Forum* (1962) was a takeoff on Roman musical comedy.

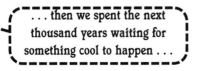

... then we spent the next thousand years waiting for something cool to happen ...

THE DARK AGES
The Middle Ages

...ZZZ...ZZZ...ZZZ...

PICK A!! PICK A!!

The Dark and Middle Ages were like a sicko's multiple-choice test:

Would you rather die of?

a. The Plague
b. The Church
c. Boredom
d. All of the above

Limping Toward the Renaissance

Inspired by greed, power, and several utterly insane versions of Christianity, "the Church" killed Jews, Muslims, freethinking Christians—and nonconformism of any kind. That lasted for several bloody centuries until the 14th century, when the rise of the great city-states of northern Italy brought the brain-dead Middle Ages to a halt. What little musicky drama existed during the Middle Ages revolved around religion. Priests and nuns mounted Christmas and Easter plays that, when combined with Gregorian chants, became what is called **pre-operatic**.

The "Quem Quaeritis" Plays

The most famous of the pre-operatic church dramas is the **Quem Quaeritis** play (*quem quaeritis* means "Whom do you seek?"). In these Easter-week plays, a group of women go to the tomb to anoint Christ's body. At the tomb, an angel asks them whom they seek. When they say they seek Jesus, the angel tells them that Christ has risen from the dead. This brief encounter was staged and sung. Other characters were added. Eventually it presented the whole story of Christ's crucifixion, all or mostly sung.

As these plays evolved they became less religious and more theatrical. They began to include figures like bawdy devils, which became so popular with audiences that the bishops ordered the plays removed from the church and into the village marketplaces. Finally, after centuries of hibernation, people began to wake up.

They call their awakening "**the Renaissance**"—the Rebirth.

To them, it was a return to ancient Greece.

THE RENAISSANCE
Italy

Italy was the home of **Michelangelo** and **Leonardo**. Italy was the place where **Vivaldi** hid in a monastery in fake monkhood just so he could write a few hundred hit tunes. Italy was the stomping-ground of princes and popes. Italy was a place where rich guys with time, money and brains made grand plans to perfect man and beautify the world. No two ways about it:

Italy was the heart, soul and pocketbook of the Renaissance.

The Camerata Group

The **Camerata** group, sponsored by Count **Giovanni Bardi**, was founded in Florence Italy in 1573. The group—composed of scholars who were also poets, singers, musicians ("Renaissance men") met regularly to rap about Greek culture. In no time, they came up with a nifty theory: *If you combine serious Drama with serious Music, you enhance the power of both.* The Greeks "borrowed" from the Egyptians, the Italians "borrowed" from the Greeks (then Wagner takes credit for everything). Count Bardi, on a roll, commissioned his Camerata group to produce a modern version of the ancient Greek art form.

The First Real Opera

In 1597 **Jacopo Peri**, with a **libretto** (words/story/text) by **Ottavio Rinuccini**, wrote *Dafne* (based on the Greek myth of the unfortunate lady who turned into a tree). *Dafne*, the first "modern" opera, was an instant success. The music has been lost, but from all accounts the music was secondary to the play, a relationship that continued through the early years of opera.

To opera's early masterminds, the story was far more important than the music.

The Earliest Surviving Opera

The earliest surviving opera—also by **Peri** and **Rinuccini**—was *Euridice*, composed in 1600.

The people went crazy for it. Opera quickly spread from Florence to Rome, Venice and all the other major cities in Italy.

Everyone loved it!

(Well, not quite everyone...)

In 1697, Pope Innocent XI ordered an opera house burned to the ground.

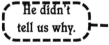

He didn't tell us why.

SCENE 2:
EARLY COMPOSERS—
1600-1800

MONTEVERDI:
The People's Genius

Opera changed drastically once it moved to Venice and into the hands and heart of **Claudio Monteverdi** (1567-1643). Monteverdi wrote his first opera, *Orfeo*, in 1607. The text (by **Striggio**) was similar to that of the old Camerata group, but Monteverdi, an authentic genius, wrote real music. The old rascal even included a few dances!

The first public opera house (**San Cassiano**) opened in Venice in 1637. There, Monteverdi could work for large groups of people instead of a few filthy rich Greek wannabes that dominated the Camerata group. The large audience of "real" people made it clear that they didn't like the talky version of opera (called **Arioso**):

- They wanted **music**—even if it delayed the opera's action!

- They want **songs**—even if they stopped the story dead!

- They wanted **fancy** songs—even if the words often couldn't quite be understood!

His audience was more important to Monteverdi than some Sugar Daddies' academic theories, so he shifted the emphasis from Dramatic Action to more Musical Opera. By 1670 there were public opera houses in Florence, Rome, Genoa, Bologna and Modena—*and 20 in Venice*—which, thanks to Mr. Monteverdi, had become the opera capital of the world. Two of Monteverdi's Venetian operas survive: ***Il Ritorno d'Ulisse in Patria*** (1639) and ***L'incoronazione di Poppea*** (1642).

Recitativo

Aria

ARIA & RECITATIVO Opera Becomes A Singer's Art

Story—at least some semblance of it—was all that separated opera from a list of Top Twenty Tunes, so Monteverdi and his acolytes couldn't trash the story altogether. If the audience hated the talky **arioso** form, opera's early geniuses would have to come up with something to replace it.

So they did! Monteverdi and the boys, acting with the wisdom of Solomon, divided the arioso form into two parts: the **Aria** and the **Recitativo**.

An **Aria** was a real song that was sung solo.

The **Recitativo** told the story, often with only harpsichord accompaniment.

Opera was becoming a series of arias interrupted by just enough recitativo to tell the story. Opera now offered more vocal display and less serious drama. The audience loved it. What they wanted was some bodacious singing. Enter "the **castrati**," the **divos** ... the first rock 'n'roll stars. But we will save them for the section on singers. For now, let's go back to the composers and to the evolution of opera itself.

Italy was, by a Texas mile, the birthplace of opera. Nobody disputes that. But you can make a pretty good case for England being second in importance during opera's formative days. Since we are about to change countries, our point will be better made if we take a step backward in time as well.

The 'MASQUES' and the MASTER

The Italian *mascherata*, the French *masquerade* and the English **masque** were different names for a pre-operatic form of "Royal entertainment" that used poetry, dance, and music ... but no drama. They were called "**masques**" (God, I hate saying things like this) because the performers often wore ... **masks**!

Technically, the English masques had no drama, so all of this would be forgettable if it weren't for a great-souled British gent named **Henry Purcell** (1669-1695). Purcell wrote the music for many masques at the English court. The power and beauty of his best music is breathtaking.

> Do yourself a favor and listen to the aria "When I am laid in earth" from Purcell's opera *Dido and Aeneas* (1689). It is remarkable, simple, beautiful and when sung by Janet Baker, Leontyne Price or Jessye Norman, it has the astonishing, elemental purity of a Spiritual.
>
> For a dramatically different take on the aria, listen to Jeff Buckley's version. At least one of Buckley's recordings of the piece is quite wonderful-probably because he doesn't try to sing it like an opera aria. He knows it's just music-alr.

- - - - - - - - - - - - - - - - - -〔 What the hell-as long as we're in England... 〕

HANDEL:
Havin' It Both Ways

George Frederic Handel (1685-1759) was born in Germany, studied music in Italy, then swam over to London (1710), where he became the most successful writer of Italian **Opera Seria** of his time. Handel wrote 35 operas for London, each filled with the impossibly difficult coloratura arias that the castrati loved to show off on ... and that the public loved. His operas *Rinaldo* (1711) and *Alcina* (1735) achieved great success with London audiences.

Haunted by Greek Tragedy

Handel wasn't satisfied with writing operas that would show off his Cadillac-without-an-engine singers. He also wrote operas that sustained dramatic interest and featured characters that the audience could admire. In the words of critic Donald Grout:

> Handel's dramatic creations are universal, ideal types of humanity... If his characters suffer, the music gives full, eloquent expression to their sorrow....
>
> We are moved by the spectacle of suffering, but our compassion is mingled with pride that we ourselves belong to a species capable of such heroism.

For a magnificent illustration of Handel's "nobly suffering characters" check out **Jan Peerce** singing the aria "**Total Eclipse**" from Handel's opera *Sampson*. (The "nobly suffering character" eliciting "our compassion mingled with pride that we ourselves belong to a species capable of such heroism" is at the heart of Aristotle's monumental definition of Greek Tragedy. The suffering is always mitigated by a sense of heroic rightness and inevitability.)

Van Gogh's Other Ear

Whether Handel's operas did or didn't achieve the stature of Greek tragedy, they were fabulously popular in 18th-century London. Handel was a natural showman. He used every stage spectacle he could beg, borrow, build or steal. His use of the orchestra was impressive. And he wrote the most dazzling bouquet of arias that anyone had ever heard, from the simple, austere and simply beautiful to the flashiest, show-offiest, most fiendishly difficult arias for singers of every voice.

With Handel, Music had achieved its primacy. It's no accident operas are "written *by*" the person who wrote the Music. The poor schlemiel who wrote the **words** is flushed down history's toilet alongside Shakespeare's wife and Van Gogh's other ear.

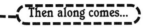
Then along comes...

CHRISTOPH WILLIBALD GLUCK
The First of Opera's Arty-Farty 'REFORMERS'

By the mid-17th century, Vienna had become so cracked for Italian opera that the Austrian royalty imported their own Italian court composers, singers and musicians. When they ran out of *real* Italians, they settled for Germans who *pretended* to be Italians! (Swear to God. You can't make this stuff up!)

By the 18th century, the Viennese, like all of Europe, were grooving on the fact that opera had become an outrageously spectacular *singers'* art.

However ... one of the imported Germans was an earnest cat named **Christoph Willibald Gluck** (1714-1787). Mr. Gluck is usually referred to by opera historians as a "**reformer**"—a word you normally use to describe prison wardens or saints on a mission from God. The no-nonsense Mr. Gluck seemed to be personally offended by the fact that the Italians had allowed opera to degenerate into mere Music.

Not even music! **SINGING!** Fancy, schmancy singing!

And can you imagine who perpetrated the Fancy Singing?

An Army of Singing Eunuchs!

Here we go again...
DRAMA!
MUSIC!

Commander Gluck wanted the Poetry and Drama of opera to reflect the simplicity and power of Greek tragedy. He hated the hot-dog singers and their excessive vocal ornamentation. In his operas *Orfeo ed Euridice* (1762) and *Alceste* (1767), Gluck tried to bring the quiet restraint of Greek drama into Viennese opera. Opera, from day one, had been a balancing act—or a *war*—between Drama and Music. As a rule, the Germans have lined up behind Drama and the Italians have formed a messy circle behind Music.

Fortunately, there are exceptions to every rule ...

> **WHOA! Let's stop for a second and take a Sanity Break.** Here, as in some other parts of this book I am sort of "riffing wise-crackingly" on the pontifications of certain self-appointed Experts. In truth, the various opinions that one 'school' of opera is more praise-worthy than another have nothing to do with how I or anyone I know got started listening to opera, or how we progressed from one kind of opera to another.
>
> You could describe my approach to opera as a sort of a minute-to-minute hedonism: if I love five minutes-worth of a piece of music, I listen to it. If I love a 20-minute piece, I listen to it. If I love the whole opera, I listen to it.
>
> Like every "convert" to opera I know, I got started listening to arias sung by a favorite singer or two. Those arias included (and still include) arias and other excerpts from operas by Gluck.

As I was saying ...
Fortunately, there are exceptions to every rule ...

MOZART:

If you had to choose one person who most gracefully combined both the Italian and German approaches to opera by the end of the 18th century, by near-unanimous agreement, it would be **Mozart**.

Wolfgang Amadeus Mozart (1756-1791) was born in Salzburg, Austria on January 27. A couple weeks later he was writing his own music. Of course I exaggerate, but only a little. By the age of five, Mozart played both the violin and the clavier. By age six he could memorize a piece of music after one hearing and had already begun composing his own music. He wrote his first opera when he was 12 years old. And so on.

Austrian Emperor Josef II *liked* Mozart's music but *loved* the music of court composer, **Antonio Salieri**. Musicologists generally consider that proof that Emperor Joseph was a tasteless bozo.

Although he died at age 35, Mozart had an impact on three separate Operatic Genres: the **Singspiel, Opera Seria** and **Opera Buffa.** Several of his operas are so timelessly musical that they are still performed today.

SINGSPIEL

The *singspiel*, "singing play," is a German version of the Broadway musical comedy, with spoken text and musical numbers. Two of Mozart's most beloved operas—*The Abduction from the Seraglio* (1782) and *The Magic Flute* (1791) —are **Singspiels.**

OPERA SERIA

Mozart also wrote in the two most popular opera forms of his day, **Opera Seria** (serious) and **Opera Buffa** (comic). *Idomeneo* (1781) and *La Clemenza di Tito* (1791), like all Opera Seria, are considered somewhat "artificial" by today's standards, but operatic styles go in and out of fashion (like everything else). Both *Idomeneo* and *Clemenza di Tito* are resurrected every decade or so by some energetic opera company and we are reminded that they contain some strikingly elegant music.

It's Mozart. Why are we surprised?

OPERA BUFFA

The operas generally considered Mozart's greatest are his three comic operas : *The Marriage of Figaro* (1786), *Don Giovanni* (1787) and *Cosi fan tutte* (1790). Some people consider Mozart the greatest composer of operas in the 18th century (I disagree: unfashionable as it may be I prefer Handel), but it would be only a slight exaggeration to say that, when it came to opera, the 18th century had been a mere Prologue.

> Opera didn't become *Opera* until the age of *Bel Canto.*

SCENE 3:
THE BEL CANTO COMPOSERS:
Three Geniuses or Three Stooges?

BEL CANTO = "beautiful song" or "beautiful singing"

In opera the early 19th century is known as the **Age of Bel Canto.** The three great Bel Canto composers—**Rossini**, **Donizetti** and **Bellini**—developed a new kind of music that demanded a new art of singing.

The singers responded by developing new singing techniques.

At times, they even led the composers.

Making Opera Wall-to-Wall Music

The **Bel Canto** composers continued the Italian tradition of giving music, melody and voice top billing in opera. They helped liberate opera from talk by eliminating much **recitativo secco.**

> **Recitativo Secco =**
> The stuff you hear in older operas that sounds more like talking than singing; it's often accompanied by harpsichord (it sounds like a piano with mittens).

Instead of using only the harpsichord in **recitativo**, **Bellini** and **Donizetti** used a full orchestra, turning even talk to music. **Rossini**?

> Please, God, don't make me think about that maniac Rossini.

> ... maybe this is a good time to insert a Glossary. Rossini would love being interrupted!

27

GLOSSARY OF OPERA-RELATED TERMS

Aria	A "song" from an opera. It may either stop the action or advance it.
Arioso	Slightly melodic; partway between Aria and Recitative; it doesn't stop the action.
Bel Canto	(Italian, "Beautiful singing") A 19th-century school of singing & composing; the operas of Rossini, Donizetti and Bellini.
Claque	(French) People hired to applaud one singer and/or boo another
Coloratura	The most florid and technically demanding kind of singing. The term usually refers to a soprano but it can apply to any voice category.
Diva	(Italian, "Goddess") An over-the-top term for your favorite soprano.
Fioritura	(Italian, "flowering") Vocal embellishments that singers (or composers) add to an Aria.
Intermezzo	Music written for the middle of an Act, usually indicating the passage of time.
Legato	(Italian, "connected") A musical direction to tie the notes smoothly together.
Leitmotif	A short tune representing characters or ideas that reached its pinnacle in Wagner's operas.
Libretto	(Italian, "little book") The text or words of an opera.
Lieder	(German, "songs") German "art" songs, usually sung by opera singers.
Music Drama	To Wagner, conventional opera was a series of action-stopping musical numbers. Wagner's ideal was the perfect non-stop unity of Words & Music, which he called Music Drama.

Opera Buffa	(Italian, "Comic Opera") It's supposed to make you laugh.
Opera Comique	A French term, usually referring to "operas" with spoken dialogue between arias.
Opera Seria	(Italian. "Serious Opera") It's not supposed to make you laugh ... but sometimes it does.
Operetta	It has lighter music and is non-Italian (*e.g.*, Viennese Operetta or Gilbert & Sullivan)
Oratorio	A religious, opera-like composition with no action; the singers just stand there and sing.
Overture	A piece of instrumental music (usually about ten minutes long) played before the opera.
Recitative	The talk-like part of the opera between arias, duets, etc—esp. in earlier opera.
Singspiel	(German, "singing play") A German "working class" opera with spoken dialogue.
Spinto	A voice with more brilliance and power than the lighter "lyric" soprano or tenor, yet not as robust as the "dramatic" soprano or tenor.
Squillo	(Italian, "ring"—ring, as in a bell). The voice's penetrating power and "ping." If a voice sends a shiver up your spine and gives you chills, it has "squillo."
Stacatto	The opposite of Legato—each note is hit quickly and separately (like left-jabs).
Trill	The rapid alternation of two separate notes—a fancy Bel Canto trick.
Verismo	(Italian) Naturalistic opera, often violent (*Cav* & *Pag*), sometimes not (*La Boheme*).

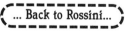
... Back to Rossini...

ROSSINI:
The Lone Ranger Meets the Marx Brothers
(Sung by Smokey Robinson and the Three Stooges)

Gioacchino Rossini (1792-1868) had the unique ability to write music that was funny and brilliant at the same time.

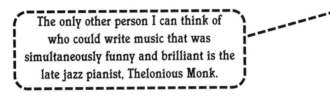

The only other person I can think of who could write music that was simultaneously funny and brilliant is the late jazz pianist, Thelonious Monk.

Rossini's comic operas, full of melody, wit and genius, include *The Italian Girl in Algiers* (1813), *The Turk in Italy* (1814), *The Barber of Seville* (1816) and *Cinderella* (1817).

ONE OF OPERA'S FAVORITE LEGENDS

Rossini wrote The Barber of Seville (arguably the greatest Comic Opera of all time?) in two weeks!

(Two Veeks?)

Yep, two stinkin' veeks!

Groucho's Serious Side

Rossini also wrote several very successful serious operas, including *Tancredi* (1813), *Moses in Egypt* (1818) and *William Tell* (1829). Rossini's comic operas are still popular but his serious operas are staged less often nowadays. Why? Maybe the 18th-century opera seria form is deservedly out of fashion. Maybe its flashy singing roles and general artificiality strike modern critics as dramatically unconvincing.

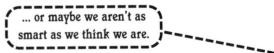

... or maybe we aren't as smart as we think we are.

LEGENDS, WISECRACKS AND DISAGREEMENTS

Legendary Meetings

Rossini dropped by Beethoven's cave to pay his respects to the deaf old Godfather of Symphony. Beethoven, who had written one dead-serious opera and was as grouchy as he looked, told Rossini to stick to comic operas.

Legendary Remarks

Rossini once said, **"Too bad I wasn't born German; I might have made something of myself."**

In every case the "quoter" took Rossini's words as a dead-serious admission that his critics were right—he was as lazy as he was talented and wasted his gifts.

I Disagree

Rossini was one of the great smart-asses of all time. There are entire books devoted to his wisecracks. I think he was busting our chops. I think it's so obvious that only a humor-impaired music critic could miss it. **(Too bad I wasn't born a critic; I might have made something of myself.)**

Groucho's OTHER Serious Side

Another of **Rossini's** contributions to opera was his use of voices in combination. The ensembles that end nearly every act of his comic operas are unmatched for sheer vitality.

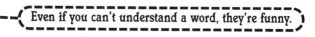
Even if you can't understand a word, they're funny.

And **Rossini's** much maligned crescendos—pure Energy! If you can sit still during a Rossini overture, you better check your pulse (that reminds me of a joke but it's a bit... it's a bit... *uncouth,* so I'll skip it)—you're probably dead.

From Sublime to Ridiculous

Mr. Rossini had about 12 different kinds of Sublime and about 150 brands of Ridiculous.

SUBLIME:	RIDICULOUS:	SIMULTANEOUSLY SUBLIME AND RIDICULOUS:
• Desdemona's long aria at the end of *Otello*—especially sung by **Fredrika Von Stade**. • The duets in *Semiramide*, sung with outrageous flair by **Joan Sutherland** and **Marilyn Horne**. • The rondo in *Moses* • Any Rossini aria sung by **Cecilia Bartoli** or **Juan Diego Florez**	• The end of every act in the *Barber of Seville*—especially the whacked-out *"Fredda ed immobile"* ("frozen with fright") bit! • The *"pappatacci"* ("eat and shut up") ensemble from *The Italian Girl in Algiers* is probably the most ridiculous piece of music ever!	• **Ugo Benelli** singing Rossini's *Messa di Gloria*—technically not an opera—it's a Mass, but it's probably the only funny Mass God ever had written to Him!

Rossini is one of those guys, like Thelonious Monk, you wish they'd done an autopsy on. They must have been Martians ... or *something*. No mere human being could have been as profoundly off the wall as those guys were.

32

DONIZETTI:
Mad Scenes & English Queens

Gaetano Donizetti (1797-1848), son of a pawnshop caretaker and a seamstress, added a dramatic urgency to Bel Canto opera that foreshadowed **Verdi** and **Verismo**. Donizetti incorporated drama into opera with greater realism than any composer of his time. While Rossini used 18th-century thoughts about heroes descended from pottery (or was that *poetry?*), Donizetti used the realistic theater of the early 19th century. As a result, many of his operas are frequently performed, especially *Lucia di Lammermoor* (1835). His operas *Anna Bolena* (1830), *Maria Stuarda* (1835), and *Roberto Devereux* (1837), loosely based on English history, are vocal and dramatic challenges, especially for the leading soprano.

> One of the most moving, beautiful, performances of opera in English is JANET BAKER singing Donizetti's *MARIA STUARDA*.

Donizetti's comedies are still performed: *The Elixir of Love* (1832) has been a showcase for every great tenor from **Caruso** to **Pavarotti**.

...And Speaking of PAVAROTTI

Donizetti's *Daughter of the Regiment* (1840) was the opera in which Big Luch hit superstardom—thanks largely to the aria in which the glorious singing fat guy hit nine high Cs!

Between Luchiano and Joan Sutherland, you had 500lbs worth of nightingale "flying" around the stage.

His Final Mad Scene

Maybe it's just a coincidence, but **Donizetti**, the composer of opera's most famous **Mad Scene** (in *Lucia di Lammermoor*), went mad and spent the last years of his life in an insane asylum.

THE 'LOGIC' OF MAD SCENES

Nothing in Opera is easier to poke fun at than Mad Scenes. Lucia di Lammermoor crashing around stage! Donizetti's cracked English queens? Bellini's ladies having nervous breakdowns onstage? What crazy purpose do they serve?

Well, actually, they do serve a purpose. Brilliant novelists (Joyce, Faulkner, Virginia Woolf, etc) used drugged, drunk, dying or otherwise "Mad" characters to "narrate" their "stream-of-consciousness" novels. Hard to imagine, but opera led the way to modern literature.

BELLINI:
If Hamlet Had Written an Opera...

Vincenzo Bellini (1801-1835) was a perfect romantic nitwit—the kind of space cadet you'd expect to write poems in a locked diary and die of unrequited love. Bellini wrote only ten operas before he bit the dust at the age of 34, but they contain some of the most purely beautiful music ever written.

His opera *Norma* became wildly popular when it was first staged in Milan in 1831 and is still going strong. One reason for **Norma**'s success is its soprano-eatin' title role, which attracts risk-takers of all kinds. It's one of the most difficult roles ever written for soprano. It demands tremendous breath control because of Bellini's long vocal line. Despite the fact that there are many fine recordings of **Norma**, it's one of those roles that is virtually "owned" by one person— in this case, **Maria Callas**.

Bellini's other operas, especially *La Sonnambula* (1831) and *I Puritani* (1835), are still staged whenever superhuman singers are available.

Maria Callas' *"QUI LA VOCE SUOA SOAVE..."* is one of the most moving arias ever recorded.

On the other hand, if there is any five minutes of singer-and-song that embodies the outrageous beauty of BEL CANTO, it is the duet from *LA SONNAMBULA*, especially as sung by Pavarotti and Sutherland ... especially the moment when Pavarotti sings "Tutto e sciolto..."

Don't look surprised; don't play dumb. You know as well as I do that Bel Canto was simply too damn beautiful to last!

SCENE 4:
VERDI... LIKE CHARLIE THE TUNA

Giuseppi Verdi (1813-1901), arguably Italy's (or the world's?) greatest opera composer, was, from his name to his music, a simple meat and potatoes guy. His name in English comes out roughly "Joe Green" and his music, at least in the beginning, was as subtle as a linebacker's hat.

The Italians called him "*Verdi bruto.*"

Verdi began by working in the Bel Canto style, but it was too pretty for him. Before long he began to develop his own style—a style simpler and more direct than the dazzle of Bel Canto.

Verdi wrote over 25 operas during his 50-year career. His work is usually divided into three periods.

The EARLY Period

His earliest works—*Nabucco* (1842), *I Lombardi* (1843), and *Ernani* (1844)—combined the rhythm and energy of Rossini with the intense drama of Donizetti and the melodic genius of Bellini.

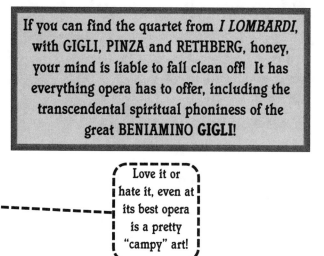

If you can find the quartet from *I LOMBARDI,* with GIGLI, PINZA and RETHBERG, honey, your mind is liable to fall clean off! It has everything opera has to offer, including the transcendental spiritual phoniness of the great BENIAMINO GIGLI!

Love it or hate it, even at its best opera is a pretty "campy" art!

The MIDDLE Period

Verdi's middle operas combine the dramatic intensity of his early period with more subtle orchestration and variation on the old Bel Canto forms. The masterpieces of the middle period include *Macbeth* (1847), *Rigoletto* (1851), *Il Trovatore* (1853), *La Traviata* (1853) and *La Forza del Destino* (1862).

Did somebody say CURSES ?

Unfortunately, even in this middle period, Verdi went weak in the knees for curses and coincidences and all the other melodramatic baloney that 19th-century theater was full of.

The two final operas of Verdi's middle period are *Don Carlos* (1867) and *Aida* (1871).

Charlie the Tuna

Near the end of his career, when he was a *very* old man, Verdi wrote two operas—*Otello* (1887) and *Falstaff* (1893). Some critics consider *Otello* and *Falstaff* Verdi's greatest operas. Most normal people consider *Otello* a bit draggy with a few wonderful arias and duets and *Falstaff* Verdi's most boring opera.

Verdi was like that old TV commercial about **Charlie the Tuna**: If you wanted opera that tasted good, you went to Verdi and the Italians.

If you wanted opera with good taste, you vent with **Wagner** and the vunderbar Germans...

The famous conductor ARTURO TOSCANINI was sitting in on a rehearsal of Wagner's *Tristan und Isolde*. During the looong love duet in Act Two, TOSCANINI turned to the woman next to him and said:

"If they were Italians, they would already have had seven children."

SCENE 5:
RICHARD WAGNER:

Genius of Music Drama?
Boring Megalomaniac?
BOTH?

BACKGROUND:
Mr. Beethoven & Mr. Weber

In 1805, the smiley Mr. **Beethoven** wrote his only opera, *Fidelio*, which inspired **Carl Maria von Weber** to write <u>German</u> operas—*Der Freischutz* (1821) and *Oberon* (1826)—based on <u>German</u> fairytales, <u>German</u> folk music and, above all, <u>German</u> theories.

(They weren't racists, they just thought they were better than everyone else.)

That's where Wagner comes in.

DER BLUES BROTHERS

Richard Wagner (1813-1883) was born the same year as **Verdi** (but seemingly in a different century).

Wagner loved theories.

(He must've wondered how the weird Italians could write an opera without a theory behind it?)

In 1849 Wagner wrote "The Art Work of the Future."

In 1851 he wrote "Opera and Drama." Wagner vent forth preaching the gospel of Music Drama.

I imagine **Weber** and **Wagner** as John **Belushi** and Dan **Ackroyd** in the Blues Brothers:

DER BLUES BROTHERS

"HI! WE'RE ON A MISSION FROM GOD."

COSIMA Liszt /von Bulow/Wagner

You may have heard stories claiming that **Wagner** was an arrogant, anti-Semitic windbag. They're all true. And then some. He sponged off of a guy named **Hans von Bulow**, then stole his wife, **Cosima** (the daughter of the composer/pianist/stud **Franz Liszt**).

Wagner and **Cosima** got carnal while still living in the supernaturally passive **von Bulow**'s house.

> Remarkably enough, Wagner found time to write an opera or two.

In 1843 he wrote *The Flying Dutchman*. In 1845 he wrote *Tannhauser*. In 1850, *Lohengrin*. In 1865, *Tristan und Isolde*. In 1868, *Die Meistersinger von Nurnberg*. In 1882, *Parsifal*.

But it was the four-opera *Ring Cycle* that gave him his rep.

That and **Cosima** Lizst/von Bulow/Wagner.

YOU RAAAANG?

> (Maybe it's just me, but for the life of me I can't imagine cuddling up with Cosima Wagner. A bit chilly, she was. (I'm trying to be nice here!)

The RING OF THE NIBELUNGS

In 1848 Wagner began the **Ring Cycle** of four operas (music-dramas)—

- Das Rheingold

- Die Walkure

- Siegfried

- Gotterdammerung

Wagner's four-opera *Ring Cycle* premiered in **Bayreuth** in 1876. That takes some 'splainin'...

BAYREUTH

At the time **Wagner** finished his **Ring Cycle**, there was no opera house in the world excellent enough to perform it (or big enough to hold his ego), so Wagner conned King Ludwig of Bavaria into building an opera house especially for him in **Bayreuth**. To "Wagnerians," **Bayreuth** is a holy place where, every year, they make the pilgrimage to see, hear and experience hours of Little Richard's operas.

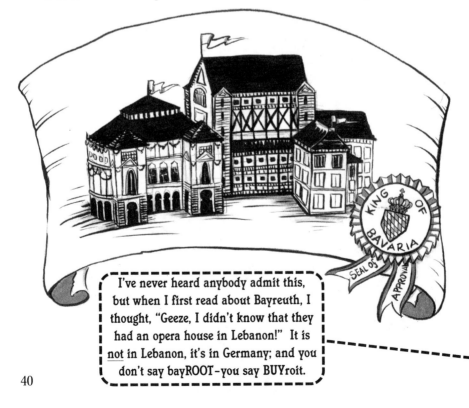

> I've never heard anybody admit this, but when I first read about Bayreuth, I thought, "Geeze, I didn't know that they had an opera house in Lebanon!" It is not in Lebanon, it's in Germany; and you don't say bayROOT—you say BUYroit.

How GOOD is Wagner?

J.L. DeGaetani (critic):
"The Ring Cycle is the greatest achievement in the history of Opera."

George Bernard Shaw **championed Wagner for years. Then Shaw changed his mind with a vengeance!**

Nietzsche—**same as GB Shaw, but even more so. He considered Wagner a danger to humanity.**

Rossini:
"Wagner has good moments but bad quarter-hours."

Bottom Line

I once spent most of a weekend listening to his entire Ring Cycle. Music, commentary, interviews—probably about thirty hours total. Once you get into it, you want to know as much as you can about both the music and the man. So after years of listening, reading and writing about Wagner and his music, I knew quite a lot about him. Despicable guy, huge ambition, manipulative, insanely anti-Semitic, self-pitying. And, as you listen to his operas, his pet techniques—like Leitmotifs (bits of music within the opera that signify certain characters or ideas; another technique that originated in opera and inspired modern novelists like James Joyce)—begin to sound so heavy-handed and obvious that you wonder why anyone would care about him or his music.

Then, by the time it's over, which ends with Brunnhilde's Immolation Scene and a whole tidal wave of motif-laden music, I sit there overwhelmed. The composer has summed up the whole world in his four-opera Ring Cycle, despite the fact that the man is a jerk.

And I keep thinking, despite myself, that I would love to teach a class that I would call "Wagner and the Limits of Art." The ultimate point being—nothing that I or anyone else can say about Wagner's Ring Cycle amounts to anything more than a grain of sand compared to that monumental Work of Art.

(The only other thing I can say that about is Toni Morrison's majestic novel, *Beloved*.)

My Bottom Line on Wagner: The man was a self-absorbed, unprincipled [*insert synonym for jerk*] whose music will bore you, infuriate you and, often against your will, raise you to heights of grandeur and the Sublime ... whether you believe in them or not. Wagner was one of the greatest composers and worst human beings of all time.

> "The French are the wittiest, the most charming and the least musical race on earth."
>
> Stendhal (1783-1842)

SCENE 6: FRENCH DUDES

Forced to Depend on the Talent of Strangers

By the beginning of the 19th century, opera was the most popular entertainment in Europe; and Paris had become its center. There was, however, a teensy weensy problem: the French, who were so gifted in painting, poetry and porn, couldn't seem to get the hang of writing operas, so they imported Italians like Giovanni Battista Lulli and advertised them/him as the "French composer, **Jean-Baptiste Lully**."

At the end of the 18th century, the extremely Italian **Luigi Cherubini** (1760-1842) settled in Paris and wrote several successful operas, most notably **Medea** (1797), a magnificent opera we might never have heard if it weren't for mighty Maria Callas. (See chapter on **Singers**).

French GRAND Opera

When the French finally did get the hang of writing opera, critics everywhere moaned. The hodge-podge they created, known as "**French Grand Opera**," was a cross between Barnum & Bailey, talky opera and ballet.

BALLET? YES, Ballet!

Lully is usually "credited" with starting French Grand Opera, but it was **Giacomo Meyerbeer** who "perfected" it in **Les Huguenots** (1836) and **Le Prophete** (1849).

Charles Guonod (1818-1893) wrote the extremely popular opera **Faust** (1859), and the slightly less popular **Romeo et Juliet** (1867)—which, as one bitchy critic put it, "suffers from the musical tastes of the day."

LAUGH and CRY

Jacques Offenbach (1819-1880), the enormously successful writer of witty, irreverent operettas, took a shot at respectability (*and hit immortality!*) by writing one semiserious opera, *Tales of Hoffmann* (1880).

Jules Massenet (1842-1912) composed several sentimental but extremely listenable operas. At least two of them, *Manon* (1884) and *Werther* (1892), are still performed today.

A Word or Two in Defense of French Opera

Virtually ALL newcomers to opera begin by listening to opera ARIAS- essentially one "song" at a time. If, like 98% of opera virgins you begin by listening primarily to arias sung by your favorite singers, arias from French opera are often wonderful, beautiful, spectacular and provide some of the most thrilling singing you'll ever hear.

Virtually all of the grouching about the tackiness of French opera comes from critics who would never admit to listening to one aria at a time.

BERLIOZ: The Godfather of Snobbery

Hector Berlioz was the first in a line of French composers whose music was not so much *written* as it was *orchestrated*. Like Wagner and his army of musical "reformers," Berlioz was on a mission from God to stomp out the Italians who were undermining the world by filling it with beautiful music. No need to take my word for it. Here is Berlioz hizself:

On arriving in Milan, out of a sense of duty, I made myself go to the latest opera [Donizetti's L'elisir d' amore].

I found the theater full of people talking in normal voices, with their backs to the stage. The singers, undeterred, yelled their lungs out in the strictest spirit of rivalry. People were gambling, eating supper in their boxes, etc.

Music for the Italians is a sensual pleasure and nothing more. They want a score that, like a plate of macaroni, can be assimilated immediately without their having to think about it...

—From the snooty *MEMOIRS* of Hector Berlioz

CONFESSION: In opera (as in Rock, R&B, or Jazz), my likes and dislikes have as much or more to do with the singer than the song—or opera. As far as I'm concerned, Berlioz is a real snorer. However: if you get **Jessye Norman** and **Placido Flamingo**, both at the peak of their glory, singing *Les Troyens* (1858), suddenly **Berlioz'** foppish music becomes supercharged , dramatic, thrilling. But, hey: **Norman** and **Domingo** in peak voice could sing the Ingredients off a cereal box and sound supercharged, dramatic, thrilling.

The seven French composers I've mentioned don't add up to Verdi's shoe or a Wagner's hat. Oddly enough, France's greatest contribution to opera was not operatic— it was literary.

SCENE 7:
'VERISMO':
TRUE-TO-LIFE OPERA

...or, anything that happens in Sicily.

The French, like the Americans, periodically show great concern for poor and victimized people. And, like the Americans, they seldom do anything practical for them. Instead, they paint pictures of them, study them like bugs in a jar or write books about them. Toward the end of the 19th century, French novelists like Zola and Merimee created a new literary style referred to as "**realism**" or "**Naturalism.**"

Offhand, you might think that a realistic novel would be about normal, average people. Ha! Naturalistic novels, and the operas that resembled them, were full of murder, revenge, rage.

They were usually about "the underbelly of society."

You mean like gypsies!

The MOST FAMOUS French Opera

In 1874, after a mediocre start as a composer, **George Bizet** (1838–1875) wrote **Carmen**, the most famous of all French operas, and the first "**naturalistic**" opera. A few Naturalistic French operas followed (like **Charpentier**'s *Louise* [1900]).

But it wasn't the French whose creative fires were ignited by **Naturalism**.

CAV & PAG
Realism ('Verismo')
Italian style

If there is any single work that defines opera to most normal people, it is almost certainly *I Pagliacci*. If you decide to open your mind (& wallet) enough to actually go to the opera house to see *I Pagliacci*, what you'll almost certainly find is a double-bill—referred to by opera addicts as *Cav & Pag*.

Cav is *Cavalleria Rusticana*, an opera that, like *I Pagliacci* (as Yogi Berra would say), is so famous that nobody goes to see it anymore.

CAV

Pietro Mascagni (1863-1945) studied at the Milan (Italy) Conservatory under the famous composer **Ponchielli**. **Mascagni** was a free spirit who hated the formal discipline of the famous music school, so he left the Conservatory to join a touring opera company. In 1890, at the age of 27, he won first prize in a contest sponsored by the music publisher Sanzogno with his one-act opera, *Cavalleria Rusticana*, based on a famous Sicilian tale by **Giovanni Verga**, featuring a jilted lover, dishonor, revenge and lots and lots of blood. **"Stark, naked passion, expressed in unabashed violence"** is how one book puts it.

Almost overnight, *Cav* was in demand all over the world, with premieres at opera houses throughout Italy, Moscow, Vienna, Madrid, Stockholm—you name it! Opera houses in New York actually had bidding wars for the rights to the first US performance.

PAG

Ruggero Leoncavallo (1858-1919), an ambitious Neapolitan (from Naples, not three-colored) composer who had been working hard without much luck, struck it rich in 1892 with this opera *I Pagliacci*, a story where Caruso catches a baritone sneaking around with his wife, so he kills both of them in an outpouring of blood, tears and melody.

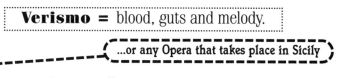

...or any Opera that takes place in Sicily

Both **Leoncavallo** and **Mascagni** wrote other operas but to most of the world, they're One-Shot-Charlies —*Cav* & *Pag*.

SCENE 8:
RUSSIAN AND SLAVIC OPERA

The Italians went into Russia and Eastern Europe, as they'd gone everywhere else, playing, writing, singing and teaching opera to anyone who'd listen. In Russia and Eastern Europe the Italians met the same fate they'd met everywhere else: they were welcomed at first as bearers of precious gifts, then resented by the "natives," who set out on a mission to de-Italianize opera, to nationalize it with their own country's myths and melodies.

After a mere 150 years of Italian coaching, the Russians began writing their own operas. And they were good ones. **Glinka, Borodin** and **Rimsky-Korsakov** wrote good operas. **Tchaikovsky's** *Eugene Onegin* (1879) is better than good and **Mussorgsky's** *Boris Godunov* (1874) can be damn near a religious experience if you get the right singer for the title role.

SCENE 9:
20TH-CENTURY OPERA

> **When choosing between two evils,**
> **I like to take the one I've never**
> **tried before.** —Mae West

Two 20th-century composers, one Italian, one German, have dominated all others: **Puccini** & **Strauss**.

PUCCINI:
Rapture of the Shallow

Giacomo Puccini (1858-1924) gets a load of bad mouth from critics, but three of his operas are among the most popular in the world:

- La Boheme (1896)
- Tosca (1900)
- Madama Butterfly (1904)

And several others aren't far behind...

- Manon Lescaut (1893)
- La Fanciulla del West (1910)
- Trittico (1918)
- Turandot (1926)

The Stephen Spielberg of opera...?

Puccini combined the Italian musicality of Verdi, a smattering of the reforms of Wagner and a great nose for what the public wanted. He was flashy but superficial—but maybe it didn't matter because the surface was so good.

He liked women, he wasn't overly encumbered by artistic principles, he drove a big orchestra and he wrote a hell of a tune. *I mean a hell of a tune!* He's the kind of guy you like better if you don't look too deep. Above all, observe the Two Don'ts:

Don't ask yourself why the women in his operas keep dying for love.

And don't ask yourself how someone that shallow can write tunes that move you to tears.

Richard Strauss—(Operas Without Men)?

When it came to writing operas, **Richard Strauss** (1864–1949) was a little bit all over the place. He wrote both mythic and realistic operas, both tragic and comic operas, and both discordant screechers and melodious Hit–Paraders.

He started out as a musical radical, with a pair of dissonant, mythic, hair–raisers: *Salome* (1905) and *Elektra* (1909).

Salome ends the opera named for her with a raving, goose–bump–inducing, several minute lust filled nervous breakdown, sung passionately to the severed head of John the Baptist!

Nekked Ladies? What Nekked Ladies? I was listening to them sing!

... and if that doesn't get your attention, MARIA EWING (they ain't all fat ladies!) did Salome's Dance of the Seven Veils with such total commitment to realism that she wound up buck nekked! I didn't see it but I read the reviews: they sounded like they were written by guys who swear they buy Playboy for the articles.

Then Mr. Strauss mellowed out with *Der Rosenkavalier* (1911) and *Ariadne auf Naxos* (1912), two nice operas with tunes you can hum (if you're **Jessye Norman**).

Hugo von Hofmannsthal

With *Elektra*, Strauss began a long collaboration with poet **Hugo von Hofmannsthal**, one of the greatest librettists (the person who writes the words) ever. In July 1929, Hofmannsthal's son committed suicide. The poet died of a heart attack on the way to his son's funeral.

The Western Obsession with German Music

I don't expect any love letters from the goons who guard the gates of the Mausoleum of Musical Theology, but for those of you who are new to classical music—or who like to make up your own minds without being conned or coerced—here is a truth you seldom hear:

Western music critics and academics—it is the fashion of the day— are not only obsessed with German music, they are utterly intolerant of anything else.

Maybe you think I'm exaggerating!

America's all-purpose, all-time cynic and smart-ass **H.L. Mencken** famously wisecracked:

> **"There are only two kinds of music: German music and bad music."**

Irving Kolodin, one of the most respected opera critics of the mid-20th century, wrote in the Preface to his *Opera Omnibus*:

"The name [Caruso] clearly gave warning of an Italian, thus of a person not be trusted with higher musical values."

In fairness to Kolodin, he was poking fun at the pro-German/anti-Italian bias that dominated the musical taste of his time—and ours. Unfortunately, he didn't realize that he never got over it!

The reason for the pro-German bias in opera was easy to understand. What we know today as "Classical Music"—*Western* Classical Music—is the result of some 500 years of invention, evolution and collaboration by composers from virtually every country in Europe (Western and Eastern), plus Russia, parts of Asia, the Americas (etc, etc). But if you had to single out one country whose composers dominated Western *instrumental* Classical Music, it would almost certainly be Germany. (What other country has a trio like **Bach**, **Mozart** and **Beethoven**?)

Perhaps the most limiting aspect of the pro-German bias isn't the way it bullies listeners, it's the invisible straight jacket it puts on SINGERS ...

> "Today's singer is appallingly restricted whether he knows it or not. From his earliest days he is subjected to all kinds of musical guidance grounded in a Germanic philosophy of the sanctity of composition and the immutability of the written note. From the beginning to the end of his career, the singer's every utterance is supervised by that 'police escort' which the virtuosos of the end of the 18th century discerned in Mozart's orchestral accompaniments."　　—Henry Pleasants, *The Great Singers*

It wasn't always that way. In the formative days, singers shaped opera right alongside the composers.

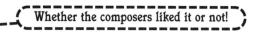

Whether the composers liked it or not!

The legendary contralto **Marian Anderson** tried for months to meet Sol Hurok (the Don King of 1930s music) but Hurok was a busy guy. One day he dropped by a concert Anderson was singing in Paris. Years later Hurok admitted how he felt when he first heard Marian Anderson's voice:

"Chills danced up my spine and my palms were wet."

ACT TWO:
OPERA SINGERS

ACT TWOOOOO

FWOMP!

Opera singers say that singing a high note is a very sexy experience. I've never sung one so I can't say. What I <u>can</u> say is that being in the same room with someone who sings one is shocking. You don't <u>hear</u> it as much as you <u>feel</u> it.

I've never been in a room with a singer anywhere near the quality of **Marian Anderson**, but let me tell you, many of the better amateur opera singers I know can make you feel things in places you never knew you had. A high note happens—or seems to happen—to every cell of you. Your toes curl, your armpits warm, and you feel sexy and spiritual and very much alive.

SCENE 10:
THE OPERATIC VOICE

CITIUS, ALTIUS, FORTIUS
(swifter, higher, stronger)
motto of the Olympic Games

Despite the arrogant diva bit, most opera singers are not only humble about their voices, they're scared witless of them. Singers generally say "the" voice, not "my" voice, as if the voice was something that didn't belong to them, something as arbitrary and moody as the Ocean.

The Voice, like love, is a gift: no matter how pretty or worthy or cool you are, you can't *earn* it, you don't *deserve* it, and it's liable to run off with the next good-looking stranger who comes along.

Mahalia Jackson put it this way: "This is not *my* voice. This is God's voice. He sings through me. And when He finishes with me, He will sing through someone else."

If you have a fair to middlin' voice, you may have some control ...

But who cares?

If you have The Voice, you don't control it, it controls you ... so you try to appease it by driving yourself crazy with lack of sex (**Del Monaco**) or you prowl around backstage like a nitwit looking for bent nails (**Pavarotti**).

FACT: Nobody knows what makes a great voice great.

FACT: Nobody knows why the Voice is "there" on Monday and gone on Tuesday.

FACT: Singing opera is so difficult, so damned-near-impossible that they should make it an Olympic sport...

Opera as an Olympic Sport?

No self-respecting opera critic could say this but, tacky dude that I am, I am free to admit that one of the attractions of opera is that opera singers can sing <u>higher</u> than anyone else. And <u>lower</u>. Not to mention, <u>softer</u>, <u>louder</u>, <u>faster</u>, <u>slower</u>. They can hold notes <u>longer</u>. They can do **trills** and **crescendos** and **diminuendos** and other phenomenally fancy tricks that "normal" singers couldn't dream of. These people are the Michael Jordans and Usain Bolts of singing.

Personally, I wish they'd make opera singing an Olympic Sport.

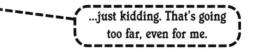

...just kidding. That's going too far, even for me.

THE OPERA VOICE—A Few Basics

Opera singers are divided into categories, depending primarily on their "range" (how high or low they can sing): Women are either **Sopranos** (high), **Mezzos** (medium) or **Contraltos** (low).

Men are **Tenors** (high), **Baritones** (medium) or **Basses** (low).

Each category is divided into subcategories, depending on the Range, Size (volume or loudness), Agility (ability to sing fast, fancy stuff), Color (hard to define things like the *brightness* or *youthfulness* or *warmth* of a voice), and, oddly enough, Emotional Disposition.

Voice teachers may be the weirdest people in the world: I knew one who, I swear, divided women into voice categories according to the size of their chests. (I left the room before he started demonstrating his technique for separating tenors from basses.)

THE CATEGORIES & SUBDIVISIONS

Sopranos

— **Coloratura**: Very high, very agile.

— **Lyric**: What most people consider a beautiful voice.

— **Spinto**: A lyric soprano with more size and intensity.

— **Dramatic**: A big, loud, emotionally intense voice...or a combination of the above (e.g., Maria Callas was a dramatic coloratura).

A role like Verdi's La Traviata makes near-impossible demands on the leading soprano: in Act 1 her role demands an agile-voiced COLORATURA; in Act 2 she must sing like a LYRIC soprano; in Act 3 her role is becomes a far more emotional DRAMATIC soprano. It's tough role.

Mezzo Sopranos

— **Lyric**: A beautiful voice (not quite as high as a soprano): Frederica von Stade.

— **Dramatic**: A deeper, darker female voice: Fiorenza Cossotto, Oralia Dominguez, Marilyn Horne.

— **Coloratura**: Instead of being a separate category, it's an "add-on" (e.g., Marilyn Horne is a Dramatic Coloratura Mezzo, but Cecilia Bartoli is a Lyric Coloratura Mezzo).

— **Contralto**: A very deep woman's voice (e.g.,Marian Anderson, Maureen Forrester, Kathleen Ferrier).

FORRESTER & FERRIER (both deceased) made magnificent recordings of songs by Gustav Mahler ("Kindertotenlieder" and "Songs of the Earth." Though technically not opera ("song cycles") they are some of the most moving "operatic" music ever recorded. As usual, Google & YouTube 'em.

Tenor

— **Lyric**: The most beautiful high male voice—often "small."

— **Spinto**: A lyric tenor with a larger, more intense voice.

> **Great Debate: Part of the game of being a tenor is "evolving" your Voice Category: thus, Pavarotti & Bjorling (etc.) both considered Lyric Tenors at the start of their careers, moved into the "Spinto" category. Spintos sing all the most famous roles. (esp. Puccini)**

— **Dramatic**: A large, strong, loud, ass-kicking male voice. Example from the past: Mario Del Monaco.

— **Heldentenor**: ("heroic tenor") a VERY loud male voice that can be heard over the huge ego—I mean orchestra—in "Wagnerian" opera. Perfect example from the past: Lauritz Melchoir.

— **Tenorino** (or Rossini tenor): A VERY high, VERY light-voiced tenor. Past: Ugo Benelli.

— **Coloratura**: As with Mezzos, is an add-on category, except for the Rossini *Tenorino*, who must have it.

Baritone

Can be divided into Lyric/Spinto/Dramatic but more often:

— **Lyric Baritone**: A pretty-voiced baritone. The word "lyric" always describes a beautiful voice. Past: Robert Merrill. Present: Thomas Hampson.

— **Verdi Baritone**: A very "studly" singer, with a powerful voice and high notes that rival the tenor's.

— **Bass Baritone:** As the name implies, a voice than either lies in the middle of the two categories, or a voice that can cover both extremes.

Two fine Bass Baritones, Bryn Terfel and Dmitri Hvorostovsky, cover that turf in different ways: Terfel started out singing lyrical German and Italian operas and songs, and has moved on to singing Wagner's Wotan, a great and demanding role. Hvorostovsky started out with Russian and Italian opera (and Neapolitan tear-jerkers!) and seems willing and able to sing anything. Unfortunately, Hvorostovsky is so preposterously good-looking that it's hard to believe the leading lady would dump him for the tenor.

Basso

— **Basso Cantante**: A bass with a lyrical, musical voice (Kurt Moll in Mozart's *Abduction from the Seraglio*).

— **Basso Profundo**: A deep, dark, sometime villainous tone. The good guy (and bad guy) in Russian opera, King Phillip (AND the Grand Inquisitor) in Verdi's **Don Carlos**. Feodor Chaliapin, Boris Christoff.

There is also a fellow called the **Counter Tenor**. The Counter Tenor is the closest thing we have to The Castrati ... speaking of which ...

SCENE 11:

"The usual procedure [allegedly painless] was to soak the boy in a very warm bath, press on his jugular vein until he fainted and then cut off the jewels."

THE CASTRATI

Somewhere around the beginning of the Renaissance, the Pope and all the other holy guys in Rome decided that women didn't belong in church choirs. However, the holy guys with the Pointed Hats noticed that church choirs without the high, beautiful voices of women sounded low and dull and stayed in the church instead of reaching up to God.

Talk about a dilemma! No normal person could have solved that problem but the Pope is a privileged man who raps with God. Whether God told him or the Pope figured it out solo, the Pope came up with an ingenious but rather grotesque solution:

The first "officially recognized" castrati (two of them) turned up in the Papal Choir in 1599.

Although the first operas were talky imitations of Ancient Greek Tragedy, when the fairly musical **Andromeda by Manelli** (1595-1667) opened at the Teatro San Cassiano in Venice in 1637, it touched off a flame that spread thorough Italy. The people didn't give a honk about a "theory" of opera—**they wanted MUSIC!**

Opera, following Darwin's law of Survival of the Flashiest, evolved toward the much more musical Opera Seria.

> **Opera Seria =** dramatically static operatic jukebox. They just stopped the action and sang at you!

The Big Three Venetians who transformed opera from a talky impersonation of Ancient Greece to a true singer's art were **Monteverdi, Cavalli** (1602-1676) and **Cesti** (1623-1669).

"You Maka Me Feeeeel..."

At the time Mr. Manelli wrote his toe-tappin' opera **Andromeda**, women were forbidden to appear onstage in Rome, and "strongly discouraged" elsewhere in Italy—like Venice. So naturally, the choir of St. Mark's (Venice) was "manned" largely by **Castrati**, the gelded gentlemen who could sing as high as any ("You maka me feeeeel...") natural woman.

So, ironic as it might seem to you Pagans, the same Catholic Church that excommunicated men who loved other men, created a situation in which men were forced to sing songs dripping with passionate romantic love ... *to other men!*

Why? Is there some deep, dark Freudian meaning hidden in there? If there is, I can't see it. The Italians were so obsessed with high voices that even after they stopped using castrati, they seemed to feel that the person with the highest voice should sing the principal role. So they stop putting castrati in heroic male roles—and replaced them with women! The result?— Trouser Roles!

> **Trouser Roles** = Roles written for women (usually mezzos or contraltos) to sing the parts of men

Trouser Roles

The practice of writing men's roles for women survived well into the 19th and 20th Centuries in operas like Rossini's *Tancredi* and *Semiramide* (roles that helped make super-mezzo **Marilyn Horne** famous), *Tales of Hoffmann* and *Rosenkavalier*.

Even the Italians, despite their well-advertised libidos, couldn't seem to get that gender business straight. When **Bellini** turned Romeo into a damsel in drag, Shakespeare must've rolled over in his (or Bacon's or Marlowe's) grave. (On the other hand, James Baldwin was probably laughing his buns off in his grave!)

(I guess it all works itself out in the end!)

But What About the Men?

Until the end of 18th Century the tenor sang secondary roles and was lucky to get an aria to himself. The bass was almost a non-entity. The Italians (truly an understatement) eventually got over their hostility toward tenors. They did such a good job of it that the Italian stock exchange now ranks tenors as one of Italy's top exports. But we're getting ahead of ourselves.

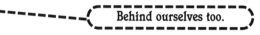

Behind ourselves too.

Ferri

The first of the great Castrati was a fellow named **Ferri** (1610-1680). Ferri was born and trained in Italy but did most of his singing in Poland! (I don't make this stuff up, you know!) By the time he appeared in Italy to sing (1643), Ferri was so famous that the townspeople met him three miles outside the city and filled his carriage with flowers (a good thing).

> **"What this noble singer expressed with his voice is beyond description. There was, to begin with, the purity of his voice and ... the impact of the trills and the ease and grace with which he achieved every note. But beyond all that, after a very long, sustained and lovely passage beyond the lung capacity of any other singer, he would, without taking a breath, go into a very long and lovely trill and then into still another passage, more brilliant and beautiful than the first."**
>
> —Bontempi, Historia Musica

The ARIA da CAPO

Opera's development was a collaboration between composer and singer. It was **Ferri's** spectacular singing that led to the **Aria da Capo**, one of the cornerstones on which opera was built.

The Aria da Capo is an aria in three parts:

- The second is a contrast to the first;
- And the third is a repetition of the first.

The popular song is derivative of the Da Capo aria.

FARINELLI: Prozac-ing the King

According to opera legend, King Philip V of Spain was so bummed out that he wouldn't wash, shave, dress or act like a proper king. The queen and her cabinet had tried all the traditional cures from leeches to Hail Mary's, so the queen, on a hunch, invited the famous castrato **Farinelli** (1705-1782) to sing a few tunes in "a room adjoining the king's apartment."

King Phil opened one eye during the first song, his other eye during the second song, and by the third song he was so moved by **Farinelli's** singing that he invited the famous gelding into his apartment and embraced him!

Farinelli did such a good job of Prozac-ing the king that every day for 25 years he had to sing the royal bozo to sleep with the same four songs. In between gigs for the nervous king, **Farinelli** managed to start an Italian opera company in Madrid.

After King Phil died (1762), **Farinelli** resumed his long-delayed tour of Europe—but by then even he could see that the reign of the castrati was coming to an end.

Things were so bad that even—God forbid—women we're beginning to appear onstage.

There is a moderately interesting movie, FARINELLI (1994), about the famous castrato. One of the more interesting challenges the film makers faced was coming up with a spectacular (or at the very least, a plausible) voice for the great castrato. Farinelli's movie voice was created by "digitally merging" the voices of a soprano and a counter tenor. The movie is part fact, all fiction, and pretty good except for the disappointing singing.

The First Women & the Last Castrati

At first Europeans were put off by the unnaturalness of women singing female roles, but eventually they got used to it. (Two early sopranos, **Bordoni** and **Cuzzoni**, used to follow each other from city to city, sabotaging each other's performances!) By the time **Velluti** (one of the last great castrati) appeared in London in 1825, the British considered *him* rather freakish.

It would take the Italians a few more years to get the message.

But when they got it, honey, they REALLY got it!

Newton merely discovered the redundant Law of Gravity. All Eisenstein did was come up with the tacky little Law of Relativity. But it was the Italians—I repeat: the Italians—who invented the TENOR!

The world had never heard anything like it.

We begin, naturally, by studying the Italian Tenor, **B.C.**

SCENE 12:
B.C. = BEFORE CARUSO

Many BC singers made important contributions to the art, skill and sport of singing opera.

In the simplest terms, these contributions fell into two categories:

- **Those who contributed to the pure SINGING of opera.**

- **And those who contributed to the ACTING.**

The UN-Altered Tenors—Pure SINGERS

Spanish tenor **Manuel Garcia** (1775-1832) had a hell of a resume: he was one of the premier tenors of his time (**Rossini** and **Donizetti** wrote operas for him); he fathered two prime time sopranos (**Maria Malibran** and **Pauline Viardot-Garcia**); he was one of the first people to "bring opera to the natives" (he toured the US in 1825); <u>and</u> he may have been the best singing teacher of all time.

People still use the instruction manuals he wrote in the early 1800s—and his only competition for the Number One Voice Teacher of all time, **Mathilde Marchesi**, was one of his students.

Despite all that, papa Garcia wasn't <u>famous</u> famous.

The reason: people had barely gotten used to the unnatural fact of women singing female roles; now, on top of that, they were expected to accept un-gelded men in male roles! (Positively unnatural!)

RUBINI

Despite the fact that tenor **Giovanni Rubini** (1795 to 1854) was awkward, ugly, had an unmagnificent voice and couldn't act, he was the first "normal" male singer to cop the kind of rock star fame that the Prima Donnas and castrati enjoyed.

Rubini did have a couple things going for him: he was the first to use the fast **vibrato**. And most important of all, Rubini invented the

ITALIAN Sob.

Think about it: no sob, no Caruso, no Gigli...no opera?

Inventing the DRAMATIC Tenor

The tenor voice is consider the most unnatural—and the most *thrilling*—of all, so it's not surprising that tenors have generally been singers first, and actors second (or not at all).

Adolphe Nourrit (1802-1839) was not your average tenor: he was an actor first, a singer second, and (if that isn't a handicap enough) he was French. He was so good that the dozen or so operas written expressly for him (by **Rossini, Meyerbeer, Halevy,** and **Auber**) literally created the repertoire for the dramatic tenor. Unfortunately, they also created the backdrop for his tragic end.

In 1837, the tenor **Duprez** made his debut at the French Opera (the place where Nourrit had reigned supreme for 12 years) in the role of Arnold in **Rossini's** *William Tell,* Nourrit's main role.

Nourrit couldn't handle it. Two years later, at the age of 37, he killed himself.

Gilbert-Louis Duprez (1806 1896) was the first tenor to sing a high C "from the chest." (All the previous ones were "head tones") How did it sound? An 1849 entry from tenor G. Roger's diary:

"Duprez, today, electrified us all .... How he hurled his guts into the audience's face! For those are no longer notes that one hears. That's his own blood, his own *life*, that he is squandering to entice from the public those cries of 'Bravo!'"

Of course that sounds way over the top, but if you hear a great singer in a great role on a good night ... that's what it sounds like. They give some of their own life, their own blood, their own soul for you. If this book serves one purpose, it is to guide you to the moments when you are overwhelmed by the beauty and power and majesty of some Singing Maniac giving his or her life blood to you.

Whether you get your bell rung by Italian opera or German opera or French opera or Music Drama or Bel Canto—it doesn't matter! The point of this book is not to help you "appreciate" opera, it is to coax you toward some of the edgiest and most intensely pleasurable moments you can have without risking your life.

Domenico Donzelli (1790-1873), Italy's first great dramatic tenor, was one of the first tenors to sing high notes without using **Falsetto**. **(Falsetto is an artificially high and sweet voice, like an operatic Smokey Robinson.)**

Rossini hated the full-voiced high notes, but he was so impressed by **Donzelli**'s singing that he wrote several operas for the man.

Defining the BARITONE & BASS

Before **Antonio Tamburini** (1800-1876) and **Luigi Lablache** (1794-1858), men with deep voices not only "didn't get no respect," they were lumped together into one indistinct category. **Tamburini** and **Lablache** defined the difference between a **Baritone** (Tamburini) and a **Bass** (Lablache).

That opened the door for the "**Verdi baritone**"—the stud with high notes that rival the tenor.

Inventing the DRAMATIC SOPRANO

Giuditta Pasta (1798-1865) was a dramatic soprano before there were any dramatic operas for her to sing. She was past her prime by the time **Bellini** and **Donizetti** wrote operas intense enough to accommodate her acting. Critic **Henry Pleasants** compares "Pasta's imperfect and unruly voice" to Maria Callas.

Maria Malibran (1808-1836), one of the first dramatic acting sopranos, toured the U.S. with her famous father **Manuel Garcia** in 1825. During that nine-month tour, Malibran, age 17, sang virtually every day without holding back. The super-intense **Malibran** died at the age of 28.

In the words of the British critic, Chorley—

"She passed across the operatic stage like a comet."

Wilhemine Schroder-Devrient (1804-1860) pioneered the *German* (as opposed to the Italian) dramatic soprano. **Schroder-Devrient** was so intense she made the Italians seem restrained. She would cry, scream, talk, rave or do anything she pleased to turn up the dramatic heat. Wagner said that seeing her in Beethoven's **Fidelio** made him decide to become a composer.) She may have been the most riveting actress ever to scream around the opera stage—<u>and</u> one of the worst singers. When she tried her hand at Italian opera, she was a graceless oaf. If you leave out the high notes and the fancy stuff like trills and cross-over dribbles, Italian **Bel Canto** opera is so smooth that it sounds like it would sing itself.

> Fat chance! Not only is it difficult to sing, but the part that sounds easiest (what singers call legato-the seamless connecting of notes) is the toughest.

Two Diametrically Opposed Approaches to the Art of Dramatic Singing

The difference between Italian and German dramatic singing is more than a difference in language, it's a difference in style, in attitude ... I am tempted to say that it's the difference between a kiss and a left-hook, but that's going too far. (<u>Not</u> a lot too far; a <u>little</u> too far.)

German dramatic opera is not so much <u>sung</u> as it is <u>declaimed</u>. "Declaim" is a polite word for <u>shout</u> or <u>harangue</u>. To *harangue* [I had to look this up] is to make a "long pompous speech characterized by strong feeling or vehement expression."

Waaay at the other end of the spectrum are the Italians, who (as one smart-ass put it) "want to sound beautiful even if the words are 'My mother is dying.'"

There is a universe between the German and Italian approaches to opera. But it's an *interesting* universe, filled with passion and brilliance and beauty on both sides.

The best illustration of the difference between the German and Italian approaches to opera can be found in two of the most famous German operas. Richard Strauss' **Rosenkavalier**, is an opera filled with great characters and lush melodies that includes a comic character—the Italian Tenor—who sings an aria intended to be SO preposterously melodic that it aims to ridicule the nameless Italian boob who sings it.

But listen to Pavarotti sing "the Italian singer's Aria (Di rigori)."

(Google **Pavarotti is THE Italian Singer** ... select "YouTube" ... and listen! Simple as that!)

And *Der Fledermaus* by Johann Strauss, probably the most famous German operetta (often performed on New Year's Eve at New York's Metropolitan Opera), features a spoof Italian tenor (Alfredo) who airheads his way through the story melodically singing his brains out no matter what the circumstances.

Rosenkavalier and *Fledermaus* are both relentlessly melodic—but when the Italian tenors enter the scene, they make everyone else sound like they are talking instead of singing.

Wagner, far too egotistical to stoop to using an Italian tenor in his Music Dramas, uses the same hyper-Melodic "Italianate" arias when it suits his purposes. When Erda sings her aria in *Das Rheingold*, her music is <u>so</u> musical that everything around it sounds like talk.

And in *Die Walkure*, Wotan spends two hours standing on a rock "declaiming" (bitching, moaning, grouching about hard it is to be King of the Gods with a Nagging Wife and a yodeling Love Child)— then launches into a beautiful Italianate aria, "*Wotan's Farewell.*" (Bass-baritone James Morris, one of the preeminent Wotans of our time was asked how he approached singing the part of Wotan. Morris said he sings it like it's Bel Canto. You can sing Wotan's Farewell like it's Bel Canto because it IS Bel Canto.)

But standing on a rock, bitching and moaning—"declaiming" in the time-honored style of Germanic dramatic singing—hard as it may be to believe, you reach a point where the "declaiming" is every bit as enjoyable as the silky Bel Canto singing.

I repeat: There is a universe between the German and Italian approaches to opera. But it's an *interesting* universe, filled with passion and brilliance and beauty on both sides.

Inventing the MEZZO

Pauline Viardot-Garcia (1821-1910), Garcia's "other" daughter, set the standard for the modern **Mezzo Soprano** through her work with the French composer **Meyerbeer**. Viardot was both a great actress and a bravura singer. If there was any complaint about her, it was that she overdid the **fioritura**.

The NIGHTINGALES

German coloratura soprano **Henriette Sontag** (1806-1854) made her opera debut at age 15. Her voice was clear, bright, high and small. Sontag was one of the few German sopranos who could challenge the Italians in their own roles—which in those days meant mostly Rossini. "My God," **Malibran** said when she first heard Sontag, "why does she sing so beautifully?"

Fioritura - a singer's embellishment of the written aria, often improvised, and considered part of every good singer's arsenal until composers began complaining-then insisting-that singers sing the aria as written, period!

(NOTE: later, when singers like Joan Sutherland, Beverly Sills and Marilyn Horne talk about returning to the art of "embellishment," this is it!)

Jenny Lind (1820-1887), the "Swedish Nightingale," acted like a saint—but she wasn't. Despite the fact that she never sang in either Italy or France—"for moral reasons"—she may have been the most popular coloratura soprano of her time. And if that isn't weird enough, she toured America with P.T Barnum. (Yes, <u>that</u> P.T. Barnum). She had a beautiful, girlish voice, great high notes, amazing breath control and a Little-Bo-Peep act that didn't quite hide the sanctimonious bigot she really was.

A mere diva would be a relief after the Swedish Nightingale.

Diva? Did somebody say Diva?

.. the lord removed the Tenor's rib, turned it into a diva, and sayeth unto them, "Go forth, be bitchy and multiply."

Adelina Patti (1843-1919) was a pretty great singer and a very great diva. In Patti's day, divas wore fake hair, fake boobs, fake smiles and of course, false eyebrows ...

One time, a rival soprano was getting a little too much applause for Patti's comfort. Patti, who always had a plan, started to stare at the lady's face in horror.

"What's the matter?" the rival whispered.

"Your right eyebrow has fallen off!"

The embarrassed rival turned her back to the audience and removed her left eyebrow.

Unfortunately, there had been nothing wrong with the right one— and the lady played the rest of the act with one of her eyebrows missing.

Patti was a singer, period. She couldn't act her way out of a paper bag (whatever that means). As far as she was concerned, acting was the last refuge for second-rate singers. And if you weren't sure if she was first-rate singer, just ask her!:

Opera fanatics love to tell about the time the suits from Gramophone finally persuaded Patti, age 61, to make a recording. Playing her records back to her was risky—whatever age she claimed that <u>she</u> was, her <u>voice</u> was 61 years old. When her records were released, many of her fans were disappointed. Not Patti. When she finally heard her own voice, she was overcome with emotion.

Blowing kisses into the playback horn, she cried,

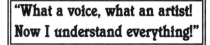

"What a voice, what an artist! Now I understand everything!"

The Queen of DIVA

Dame Nellie Melba (1861-1931), never the shy type, called herself the Queen of Song. The Australian Soprano was witty, bitchy, and power hungry (those were her good qualities).

But she could sing. **Mary Garden**, a rival Soprano who had every reason to hate her, said of **Melba's** high C in a performance of *La Boheme*, that:

> **"...it came over like a star and went out into the infinite. My God, how beautiful it was!"**

There is a famous story involving **Melba**, tenor **Jean de Reszke** and ... I'll let Melba tell it:

> **"I shall never forget an evening when I was singing with Jean de Reszke [Chicago, 1896] in Romeo and Juliet ... and before I knew what had happened I saw clambering up over the footlights a man with staring eyes and the face of a lunatic, coming toward me.**
>
> **It was a lunatic, a man who had in some way or other escaped from his asylum and had obtained entry to the house. For a moment everybody was paralyzed. And then Jean came to the rescue. He ran forward, drawing his stage sword from its sheath and waving it fiercely in the man's face. The man looked as though he might give fight–and if he had done so I don't know what would have happened, for he was a powerful fellow and a theatrical sword is not a very good weapon against the strength of a maniac."**

—Dame Nellie Melba, "Melodies and Memories," 1925

Jean de Reszke (1850-1925) was not only a brave guy, he was also one of the greatest Italian tenors of all time—despite the fact that he was Polish and specialized in French opera!

He also became one of the great *German* tenors when he did the unthinkable and became a Wagnerian heldentenor (heroic tenor) late in his career. **De Reszke** was a hard act to follow.

That's where the little fat guy from Naples comes in...

75

Caruso, when he was an unknown tenor, auditioned for Puccini by singing "Che gelida manina," from Puccini's La Boheme. Puccini, stunned, said, **"Who sent you—God?"**

SCENE 13:
MR. CARUSO

Why, you may reasonably wonder, should opera singers be divided into BEFORE and AFTER **Caruso**—with Uncle Enrico in the middle like the Mason-Dixon line?

Caruso may have been the greatest opera singer of all time (or the greatest tenor) (or the greatest Italian tenor). You can argue about that till your fake eyebrows fall off. It's a matter of taste that even you will change your mind about several times.

That is NOT the reason Mr. Caruso is the dividing line.

These are the reasons:

Caruso changed the art of opera **singing**

Caruso changed the art of **being** an opera singer

But above all, because from Caruso onward, you can **hear** the singers we're talking about.

We are not talking about anything mystical here; the Singers were **recorded**!

One thing you have to love about Caruso is that he broke so many stereotypes.

Breaking the Stereotypes

Take for example, the common presumption about opera being a rich person's sport ...

Enrico Caruso (1873-1921), arguably the greatest opera singer of all time, was a little fat guy from the slums of Naples. He was the 18th of 21 children, only three of whom lived beyond infancy. As a boy, he worked in a machine shop to help his family survive. Evenings, he sang on street corners to earn money for singing lessons.

Caruso made his debut in Naples in 1894 in an opera that not only flopped—it *disappeared*! He was 21. Two years later, he materialized at **Puccini**'s crib. Two years after that, he created the role of **Loris** in **Giordano's** opera *Fedora*. Two years after that, he made his debut at **La Scala**, the opera house in Milan where they make you "keep singing, until you get it right." (He got it right the first time.)

HIS MASTER'S VOICE

In 1902, one of the pointmen from Gramophone heard **Caruso** singing up a storm at **La Scala** and was so astounded that he offered the tenor $500 to record ten arias. The head office wired back, **"Fee Exorbitant. Forbid You To Record."** The guy ignored his bosses, and the records made a fortune—that, my brothers & sisters, is how supernatural the chubby brother's voice was! That big, lush, perfectly focused voice of his was pretty much the only voice in town that could move the Flintstone technology of the old Gramophone and Victrola recording machines. Other beautiful voices came out squeaky or muffled; Caruso's voice sounded like God was singing in your living room!

Caruso's recordings were not considered "collector's items" in any serious sense simply because he sold zillions of them! Caruso was a pop recording artist—**Elvis the Pelvis Caruso!**

> PLEASE NOTE: From the age of Caruso-around 1900-until the present, thanks to the miraculous gift of the Internet, you can hear virtually any singer, past or present, for FREE!
>
> Just Google the singer's name, follow the option to YouTube, and select any aria or opera you're curious about.

The Down to Earth DIVO

In 1903, at age 30, **Caruso** made his American debut at "the **Met**" (Metropolitan Opera House) in New York. Americans loved him. Not only was there that Voice, but he fit in perfectly with America's notions (or fantasies?) of democratic equality. The Greatest Singer in the World—and he's a nice guy! Talk about breaking stereotypes. Nice, likeable, warm, generous (to a fault)—even approachable. He was the perfect American success story. So what if he was Italian? Everybody in America is *something*!

Yes, but...How Did He Change the Art of SINGING Opera?

Caruso was to singing what **Verdi** was to composing: he made singing more direct, simpler, less fancy, more blatantly emotional. He premiered many of the most famous tenor roles in operas by **Puccini**, **Giordano**, and **Cilea** and his performances in Verismo operas (e.g., *Pagliacci*) are still the standards by which tenors are judged. According to some smart cookies, what made **Caruso's** voice so unique (and gave it that magnificent organ-like resonance) was that his "**chest voice**" was as beautiful as his "**head voice**." (Approximate Popular Music equivalents from old R&B days: "Head Voice" = Tony Williams of the Platters; Chest Voice = late R&B great, Jackie Wilson. For those of you who'd like to hear either or both of those great Soul Singers, just go to YouTube.)

The Caruso sob is also definitive.

On the OTHER Hand

Stefan Zucker (formerly of "Opera Fanatic" magazine and radio show) believes that Caruso, in some ways, had a negative impact on the art of singing opera. According to Zucker (and the man is a veritable compendium of opera knowledge), Caruso was the first to sing without "dynamic modulation" (mixing loud and soft singing.) Caruso was the first to sing almost exclusively "forte" (loud).

Music to DIE For

Caruso stayed at the Metropolitan Opera for 18 years, where he sang over 600 performances in 40 different roles. Caruso was so reliable that he hardly ever missed a performance, so everyone in attendance was shocked to see him in trouble during a performance of *L'Elisir d'amore* at the Brooklyn Academy of Music (December 11, 1920). Caruso was spitting blood with every phrase, but he kept singing. His doctor hysterically waved at him to stop, but he kept singing. Finally, the General Manager of the Met was called in to stop the performance. Everybody in the audience knew that they'd witnessed an extraordinary act. But what did it mean? One of the most gifted men the world has ever known was risking his gift, his Voice—maybe even his <u>life</u>—to sing opera. Can the music be that important?

Two days after his Brooklyn performance, Caruso sang in *La Forza del Destino*. He sounded as good as ever; he tried to put the pain out of his mind. He sang *La Juive* on Christmas Eve, but he couldn't hide the pain on his face. The next day, during a Christmas party, the pain attacked again. It was diagnosed as pleurisy.

He had an operation. He lost weight. He died.

Can the music be <u>that</u> important?

Is there something going on here that we don't understand?

Yes. We'll get to it.

SCENE 14:
A.C. = AFTER CARUSO
(EARLY 20TH CENTURY—BETWEEN CARUSO & CALLAS)

There were so many fine singers at the turn of the century that the period between 1890 and 1920 is called the "Golden Age" of singing.

American superstar soprano **Geraldine Farrar** (1882-1967) was pretty, she was often paired with Caruso, and she was a better singer than she's usually given credit for. (Her recording of "*Vissi d'arte*" from Puccini's *Tosca* has a rhythmic drive that few other singers managed.)

Mary Garden (1874-1967) was born in Scotland, raised in Chicago, and specialized in French opera.

Titta Ruffo (1877-1953) was the baritone Caruso. They didn't exactly avoid each other, but it was no accident that Ruffo made his American career in Chicago and they recorded together only once— the duet from Verdi's *Otello*. Caruso's voice, always magnificent, became darker and more baritonal as he aged. By the time he sang that duet with Ruffo, you could barely tell them apart.

The great Irish tenor **John McCormack** (1884-1945) was as unlike Caruso as a tenor could be—McCormack's voice was high and thin and very Irish—but he and Caruso admired each other so much that each called the other "the world's greatest tenor."

Amelita Galli-Curci (1882-1963) was a tiny, hummingbird-voiced coloratura who could sing circles around the Big Mama's. (There is a bizarre recording alternating Galli-Curci's little flute-like singing voice with her 75-year-old croaky speaking voice.)

Speaking of big mamas, **Ernestine Schumann-Heink** (1861-1936), was an extremely big mama, a contralto who was born in Czechoslovakia, studied music in Germany, and became a proud American citizen. **Schumann-Heink** was a life-loving earth-mother, roughly the size of a large refrigerator. About the only thing that'd tick her off is if you implied that she hadn't lost her German accent. (She made a beautiful recording of "Danny Boink.") One day the lovable linebacker boogied into an American drugstore for a few staples ...

> "I'd like some powder please," says she.
>
> "Mennen's" asks the clerk.
>
> "No. Vimmen's."
>
> "And would you like it scented?"
>
> "No, I'll take it vit me."

Always Be Sincere ...

The Italian tenor Beniamino **Gigli** (1890-1957) is generally considered Caruso's successor, although he was much different in voice and personality. Caruso's voice was always "studly," whereas Gigli's voice was not only smaller, but a little sissified. Caruso, even though his sobs were sometimes over the edge, had what contemporary tenor **Francisco Araiza** calls "a tear in the voice," whereas Gigli is clearly an impostor. Gigli is famous for many things—for having one of the most beautiful natural voices, for "covering" the voice (using the sound "aw" instead of "ah"), but what Gigli is most famous for in my heart is his Magnificent Phoniness. Gigli was so moved by his own singing that he would stand on stage, clutching his heart, sobbing for several minutes after he finished his aria.

> In the words of Harry S. Truman—
> **"Always be sincere, even if you don't mean it."**

It's NATURAL

Giovanni Martinelli (1885-1969) is usually considered next in the line of great Italian tenors. Opera lore has it that he was scheduled to replace an ailing **Gigli** halfway through the opera *Andrea Chenier*. **Gigli**, who was in resplendent voice despite his illness, sang Chenier's "*Improviso*" aria.

Martinelli said, "**You expect me to go out there and sing after that!**"

> "**A very young performer, inexperienced in the perils of the profession, made an appearance in company with the great Giovanni Martinelli. Both flattered and awed by the veteran's concern for her well-being during an embrace, she discovered—to her maidenly surprise—that she was encountering a rigid male organ poking her in the groin. As she instinctively recoiled, he squeezed her hand in a gesture of reassurance, and said, "*Perdona, signorina. E'naturale!*" ("No need to get bent out of shape, lady. It's natural!")**
>
> Irving Kolodin, *The Opera Omnibus*

To Vibrato or NOT to ...

Aureliano Pertile (1885-1952) was a star at La Scala and Toscanini's favorite tenor, but he never caught on in America or England because of his fast vibrato (the British called it "bleating").

Tenor **Giacomo Lauri-Volpi** (1892-1979) also had the characteristic Italian vibrato, but he sang at New York's Metropolitan Opera for over ten years (from 1923-1934).

Tito Schipa (1890-1965) was a fine light-voiced tenor, despite the fact that he didn't have a great voice or great high notes. All the poor guy had were brains and elegance.

> Do yourself a favor and check all of them out on YouTube.

BEAUTY and the BASS

Spanish mezzo **Conchita Supervia** (1895-1936) was the last of the great vibratos. Her career was not hurt by the facts that she had a beautiful face, a great body, sang her first **Carmen** at the age 15 and sang **Rossini** like she was born for it.

Maria Jeritza (1887-1982), star of the Vienna Opera, didn't have a thing going for her except a gorgeous voice, great acting ability, and a body that looks fat in pictures but apparently had **Puccini** sniffing around her like an old hound dog.

Ezio Pinza (1892-1957), one of the great Italian basses from the 1920s to the 1940s, couldn't read music, loved the ladies, and had one of the most magnificent voices ever.

Feodor Challapin (1873-1938), the first Russian "basso profundo" to become internationally famous, single-handedly made **Boris Godunov** part of the standard repertory in opera houses all over the world. He was a great singer and an even better actor.

Claudia Muzio (1889-1936) was a passionate singing actress, one of the first "modern" **verismo** singers. She had a beautiful, smoky voice, a strong personality, and brains.

WAGNERIAN HeldenHonkies

Lotte Lehmann (1888-1976) was one of the great German sopranos of the first half of the 20th century. She originated many of Richard Strauss' soprano roles and she sang with tenderness even when impersonating one of Wagner's helmeted heldenmamas.

Frida Leider (1888-1975), another glorious Wagnerian soprano. Leider had a bright, beautiful, youthful-sounding voice compared to most Wagnerian sopranos. She sang the fat-lady roles with a voice as clear as...as clear as...as clear as...

Friedrich Schorr (1888-1953) was one of the greatest Wagnerian bass-baritones of all time. His huge, vibrant voice glowered over Wagner's zillion-piece-orchestra like rolling thunder.

Many Jews despise Wagner, an arrogant, unrepentant anti-Semite.

Although he didn't exactly advertise it, Friedrich Schorr was Jewish. Maybe he felt that his presence was the best revenge: Schorr's signature role was Wotan, King of the Gods.

Kirsten Flagstad (1895-1962) was nobody's favorite singer until, **at age 39**, she tackled opera's toughest female role: the mighty **Brunnhilde**. She became the Wagnerian soprano of the 1930s-40s. Flagstad's performances with **Melchoir** saved the Metropolitan Opera from collapse during the Great Depression of the 1930's.

Speaking of Mr. **Melchoir:** if a singer's irreplaceability is the ultimate standard of greatness, then Danish tenor **Lauritz Melchoir** (1890-1973) is the greatest singer of all time. **Melchoir** sang all of Wagner's most brutal heldentenor roles, and in the process, showed us what beautiful music they were. He was also the top partner for all three of the Wagnerian super-ladies listed above (and others). Since **Melchior's** retirement, nobody has stepped in to fill the "helden-gap" he left. *(Siegfried, where are you?)*

Austrian tenor **Richard Tauber** (1891-1948) started out in opera but made his greatest impact in operetta. He had a unique voice that he used with outrageous flair ... and he wore a monocle!

Rosa Ponselle (1897-1981) was born in Connecticut and discovered by **Caruso**. She became one of the great Verdi sopranos and set the standard for the role of **Norma** ... until Callas came along.

Marian Anderson (1903-1993) was born in Philadelphia, where her father sold coal and her mother worked as a maid. In 1929, she went to Europe on a scholarship and met the impresario **Sol Hurok**, who signed her for a concert in Salzburg (August, 1935). Just before she was ready to go on, she was told that **Toscanini**, the Pope of conductors, might attend. She panicked, but went onstage and sang. After the concert, **Toscanini** came back stage to talk to her but she was so nervous she didn't hear a word he said. After Toscanini left, others in the room told Anderson what he'd said:

> **"Yours is a voice one hears once in a hundred years."**

It would be another 20 years before Anderson would make her debut at the Metropolitan Opera.

During that time, a lot happened, including World War II and Maria Callas.

SCENE 14: P.C. = POST CALLAS
MID-TO-LATE 20TH CENTURY

> Where had she learned it? Her vocal quality–not only the natural sound, but the way in which she used it–was so unusual that she practically had to barge into opera. "That woman [Maria Callas] will never sing at La Scala," Antonio Ghiringhelli (chief administrator of La Scala) told Gian Carlo Menotti. "Never! Never!"
>
> Ethan Mordden, *Opera Anecdotes*

Maria Callas (1923-1977) was born in Brooklyn to Greek parents. Shortly before World War II, her mother took her to live in Greece, where Maria studied voice with an unspectacular teacher and made an unremarkable debut in 1938.

Then something happened. It's as if one night in her sleep she was visited by **Rossini, Bellini, Verdi, Wagner, Puccini** and a couple dozen of the world's greatest prehistoric singers ... and ... they put a computer chip into her head? Or *something*? I know the rules; I know things like that can't happen. But it's *as if* they happened!

Suddenly, in 1947, this unremarkable girl makes a strong debut in Verona. In 1949, this ordinary girl sings **Brunnhilde** (in *Die Walkure*) and **Elvira** (in *I Puritani*)—back-to-back! (Is this girl demented? Doesn't she know that's impossible?)

Even more astonishing, this Greek girl from Brooklyn is telling the baddest conductors in Italy how **Rossini** should be sung! And **Bellini**, **Donizetti**, **Verdi**—you name it! The woman is clearly nuts. She acts like she just got back from the 18th century!

In 1951, Callas sang *Norma* at La Scala. She was so good it was scary. But she was still nuts! In Brazil, she found her name removed from posters advertising her upcoming *Tosca*, so she beat the hell out of the opera house's impresario! (In those days, Callas weighed over 200 lbs, so she carried a serious wallop!)

What **Gobbi** saw a year later, he couldn't believe: she had lost over 100 lbs and she was beautiful, but those things one accepts. What shocked **Gobbi** was that this new **Callas** was not the old one transformed. She was, or seemed to be, an entirely new person. Everything that was <u>not</u> the diva had been burned away.

Madame Butterball

It was around that time that conductor **Tulio Serafin** told **Callas** that her large body was restricting her career. **Maria** protested that she wasn't *that* big. The great baritone **Tito Gobbi** tactlessly pointed out a nearby scale. Callas weighed herself, took off her coat, weighed herself again, then stormed away.

The Great Ugly Voice

Callas' voice was so odd it's a wonder she ever got past the lobby of a big-time opera house. But it was unmistakable. Conductor **Carlo Maria Guilini** called her "**the Great Ugly Voice.**" She considered it a compliment; he meant it as one.

Between 1950 and the early 1960s Callas revived a couple dozen dead operas, revived—*and redeemed*—the entire genre of **Bel Canto** operas, changed the performing of <u>all</u> opera, and raised the sights of every opera singer who followed her. All that in a career whose prime lasted barely ten years. After the early 1960's, the wobble became wobblier and the high notes screechier.

Of course, along the way, she also dissed soprano **Renata Tebaldi**, pissed off the president of Italy (she walked out after Act One of *Norma* when he was in the audience), routinely cancelled performances and feuded with anyone dumb enough to get in her way.

Then one day the greatest, baddest opera singer since Caruso met the rich butterfly collector, Aristotle Onassis. He pinned her, told her to give up opera. She did. He married Jackie Kennedy in 1968. (If only she hadn't given up opera, we could have hated Onassis with a nice clear conscience; but she did, so we can't.) Officially, Callas didn't die until 1977.

Maria Callas
Soprano, Coluratura

AUTHOR'S NOTE: After I wrote that last line, I found myself looking up Billie Holiday's birth & death years, half expecting them to be the same as Callas'. (They aren't.) I cannot understand one without the other. Geniuses in music; self-destructive dimwits in love.

Technically, of course, there is no similarity between the voices but compare the sense of despair Callas expresses in "Qui la voce..." with the despair conveyed by Billie Holiday in "I'm a Fool to Want You." Both recordings are masterpieces of expressive singing. Isn't that what opera is all about?

When Callas sang, she put everything on the line. Did we expect her to love any other way?

The La Scala gang

The recordings from La Scala during the Callas years set the standard for other opera houses. La Scala had great conductors like Guilini and Serafin, big-time movie directors like Visconti and Zeffirelli, and enough fine singers to fill three opera houses. Two of the greatest La Scala singers were Gobbi and di Stefano.

Baritone Tito Gobbi (1913-1984) made his debut in 1937, but his career didn't really fly until after WWII. By the 1950s, he was in demand all over the world. He sang and acted with equal suavity: he could be funny (Figaro in Barber of Seville), brutal (Scarpia in Tosca), or tender (Rodrigo in Don Carlos). He sang with Callas in many of her best roles (like Tosca.)

The Italian tenor Giuseppe di Stefano (1921-2008) was Callas' most constant partner. He started out as a popular crooner before he committed his smooth tonsils to opera. He made his debut in Italy in 1946, and at the Met in 1948. It would be wrong to treat di Stefano as merely Callas' partner; he was a glorious singer in his own right. Supertenor Jussi Bjorling once said, "Di Stefano could be the best of all of us if he put his mind to it."

Jussi Bjorling (1911-1960) started singing professionally with his father and brothers at the age of six. He made his operatic debut in Stockholm in 1930. Caruso's widow said that Bjorling's was the only voice she'd ever heard that reminded her of Caruso.

That made a lot of people nervous:

In 1931 the great Feodor Chaliapin appeared in Stockholm, Sweden as a guest artist singing Mephistopheles in Gounod's Faust. The tenor on his occasion was the legendary Jussi Bjorling, then at the beginning of his career; throughout the performance, Chaliapin noticed that the young tenor had a splendid voice and might provide too much competition for him in this crucial final scene. When the time came for them all to belt it out, Chaliapin simply removed his competition by swirling his cape around the young tenor and covering him from the site (and sound) of the audience!

Stephen M. Stroff, *Opera—An Informal Guide*

Early in 1960, **Bjorling** had a heart attack at Covent Garden (London) just before the curtain of *La Boheme*. Bjorling, reputed to be a man of immense physical strength, insisted on singing because the Queen of England was in the audience. He died a few months later.

It was the year that **Leontyne Price** made her **Met** debut.

Five years earlier, in 1955—twenty years after **Toscanini** had raved about her—Met Opera general manager **Rudolf Bing** (1902-1997) defied the Met's whitebread Board of Directors and invited **Marian Anderson** to sing at the Met. She was still a fine singer, but she was well past her prime, so opera lovers never did get to hear the real **Marian Anderson**.

And they're still trying to figure out which Rudolf Bing was the <u>real</u> Rudolf Bing!

Rudolf the Blue-Nosed Impresario

The Rudolph Bing that **Callas** fans despised did the unforgivable: during **Callas'** prime (the 50s and early 60s) she sang at La Scala, Covent Garden, the Paris Opera, the Lyric Opera of Chicago ... she sang damn near everywhere in the world except the Met. Actually, she sang at the Met *twice* during her prime. She was scheduled to sing more performances, but Bing fired her because (in his words) "there was no room at the Met for a Prima Donna."

Opera lovers saw through Bing's doubletalk. What he really meant was that there was room at the Met for <u>only</u> one Prima Donna—**Rudolph Bing**!

> **Bing the Bitchy was famous for his wisecracks:**
>
> Someone remarked, [conductor] "George Szell is his own worst enemy."
>
> "Not while I'm alive," Bing replied.

As long as we're doing Bitchy Remarks

After hearing **Tebaldi**, **Callas** said, "What a lovely voice. But who the hell cares?"

However ...

You don't take the trouble to dump on someone who isn't a threat. **Renata Tebaldi** (1922-2004) grabbed some serious international fame when **Toscanini** (1867-1957) chose her for the reopening of La Scala in 1946. By 1955, she had sung in all the major opera houses. **Tebaldi** was a tame actress with a big luscious voice. Opera lovers are like sports fans: if you loved Jordan, you feel obligated to diss LeBron. **Tebaldi** fans **and Callas** fans were like rival New York gangs, complete with occasional fistfights. Each of them had "claques"—people (sometimes hired by the singers themselves) who show up at the opera house to noisily applaud a favored singer or to boo and disrupt the "enemy" singer.

Franco Corelli (1923-2003), who sang with both **Callas** and **Tebaldi**, didn't have much formal voice training but he had a big, ringing tenor voice with great high notes. Unfortunately, Corelli lived in such mortal terror of his own high notes that his anxiety over performing shortened his career. They called him "Golden Calves."

The mature American tenor Richard Tucker tried to ignore the opera house flunkies fawning over the studly new tenor, Franco Corelli. Sensing Tucker's discomfort, the disgustingly handsome, magnificent-voiced Corelli told Tucker that he admired the old dude's version of an aria from Puccini's *Tosca*. Corelli asked Tucker's advice on singing the piece.

Tucker, whose toupee look like a pancake that had been dropped on his head, said, "To sing it right, Franco, you have to be Jewish."

Mario "Iron Lungs" Del Monaco

Richard Tucker (1913-1975) was many people's second or third-favorite tenor. He sang at the **Met** for 30 years and never gave anything less than all-out performance.

Which brings us to **Mario** "Iron Lungs" **Del Monaco** (1915-1982). **Del Monaco** was the great Italian dramatic tenor of the 40s and 50s—if not, of all modern time. His specialty was the title role in **Verdi's** *Otello*. He had a fierce and beautiful voice, was almost as good-looking as **Corelli**, skipped sex before performances like a prizefighter, and sometimes got so carried away that he shouted his lines instead of singing them!

They say that Swedish soprano **Birgit Nilsson** (1918-2005) didn't drown out **Franco Corelli** when they sang *Turandot* together because she liked him. **Corelli** had a huge voice, so that would seem ridiculous unless you heard **Nilsson** sing. She was, without a doubt, the Wagnerian Soprano of the 50s, 60s, and part of the 70s.

ORCHESTRA

Her huge ringing voice rose above even the largest orchestras.

German soprano **Elisabeth Schwarzkopf** (1915-2006) made her debut in Berlin in 1938. She specialized in **Mozart** and **Richard Strauss**. Her interpretation of the Marschallin in Strauss' *Der Rosenkavalier* is still considered definitive.

Leontyne Price (b. 1927) was such a magnificent singer it is hard to imagine her not being an enormous success, but racism does have a way of making people deaf, dumb, blind and stupid—so we thank **Marian Anderson** for making **Leontyne Price** possible. Ms. **Price** was the first African-American opera singer to make an international reputation. She was born in Mississippi, studied at New York's Juilliard, and became the top **Verdi** soprano of the 60s, 70s, and part of the 80s.

Australian soprano **Joan Sutherland** (1926-2010) had a voice as big as a Wagnerian soprano and as flexible and high as a coloratura. She and her husband, conductor **Richard Bonynge** (b. 1930), took the **Bel Canto** revival in a "**Rossinian**" direction. **Rossini** believed that singers and conductors should <u>not</u> treat the composer's written score like the Bible, but that each singer should modify the music to suit her own voice and temperament. **Sutherland** and **Bonynge** started the movement in the 60s. Others, like **Beverly Sills** and **Marilyn Horne**, took up the cause.

> Richard Bonynge, Sutherland's husband and voice coach, "tricked" her into developing her spectacular high notes by telling her she was singing a B-flat when in fact, she was singing a C, D, and on up into the stratosphere.

Where **Sutherland** was an atypical big-voiced coloratura, **Beverly Sills** (1929-2007) was a traditional small-voiced type. She was a smart singer but by the time she hit major fame, her voice had lost a bit of its bloom. After she quit singing, **Sills**, the good-natured, unpretentious, hearty-laughing lady next door, became the head of the New York City Opera.

And one of opera's finest ambassadors.

If opera singers had a shootout at the OK Corral to see who can sing higher and lower and faster and slower than anyone else, I'd put my money on **Marilyn Horne** (b. 1934). She may be the greatest razzle-dazzle coloratura mezzo soprano ever recorded. And she's been singing since the 1950s, when her voice was "loaned" to Dorothy Dandridge in the movie, *Carmen Jones.*

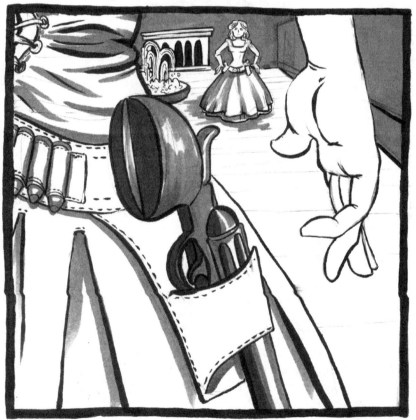

The strengths of Jessye Norman (b. 1945) are so obvious you wonder why the Met didn't hire her until 1983, *when she was 38 years old.* In her debut season at the Met, she sang the parts of both Cassandra and Dido in **Les Troyens**, and in the process she made me like the snooty **Berlioz**.

THREE TENORS

For all I know, you live on Mars and you've never heard of **Pavarotti, Domingo** and **Carreras**.

Tenor **Placido Domingo** (b. 1941) was born in Spain, trained in Mexico and sings everything—I mean EVERYTHING!—**Verdi, Wagner, Offenbach, Mozart, Berlioz**—the list is endless. He's one of the smartest singers in the world and one of the few opera singers who've actually improved with age. In the 80s he began conducting—he's good at that too. Maybe we could talk him into running for president He even, God forbid, seems sane!

In 1963, **Luciano Pavarotti** (1935-2007) was called in as a last-minute substitute for **Giuseppe di Stefano** in a Covent Garden (London) production of *La Boheme*. The next day's *London Times* read, **"Discovery of great new Italian tenor."** In 1965, he was invited to tour with **Joan Sutherland**. In 1967, he sang the **Verdi *Requiem*** with **Leontyne Price**, *at* La Scala, *conducted* by Herbert von Karajan. **Pav's** *first* debut at the Met in 1968 was a disaster—he had the Hong Kong flu. He returned to the Met in 1972, singing **Donizetti's *Daughter of the Regiment***, which included an impossible aria with nine high C's. It put him on the cover of *Time* magazine and the rest is history.

The *Time* magazine article compared Pavarotti to a "clutch" athlete who could be counted on to perform magnificently in the most nerve-wracking circumstances. Nine high C's, night after night, after boogie-ing around the stage all night like a 300-lbs puppy! Pavarotti's Met performance of *Daughter of the Regiment* was spectacular. The first eight high Cs were surprisingly tiny [in volume]. The ninth high C was powerful, ringing and resonant.

> **This opera is famous for the aria "Ah! mes amis, quel jour de fête!" (sometimes referred to as "Pour mon âme"), which has been called the "Mount Everest" for tenors. It features nine high Cs and comes comparatively early in the opera, giving the singer less time to warm up his voice. Luciano Pavarotti's stardom is reckoned from a performance alongside Joan Sutherland at the Met, when he "leapt over the "Becher's Brook" of the string of high Cs with an aplomb that left everyone gasping."**
>
> —WIKIPEDIA

Pavarotti's more serious aria in the last act of the opera ("*Pour me rapprocher de Marie*") may have been even more striking than the flashy piece with nine high Cs. One of the most remarkable things about Pavarotti is that he can murder you with either the sheer beauty of his voice (surely one of most beautiful Italianate tenor voices of all time), OR with <u>one</u> zinging high note!

He is not overrated. (I won't use the past tense on him even though he died in 2007. His recordings, which include some rarities most of us never heard during his lifetime, are alive and well on YouTube and zillions of other places.)

Try this loose-as-a-goose playful piece—a very young Pavarotti singing an aria from *I Due Foscari* ...

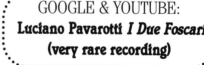

GOOGLE & YOUTUBE:
Luciano Pavarotti *I Due Foscari* (very rare recording)

Spanish tenor **Jose Carreras** (b. 1946) had a beautiful voice and looked like a movie star, so no one was surprised when he began to get "famouser and famouser." Then, in 1985, he was stricken with leukemia. After months of treatment, including a bone marrow transplant, he recovered. With incredible patience and perseverance, **Carreras** worked his way back to singing. The voice, after he recovered, was not the same. It wobbled like a wagon on a cobblestone street. But you had to respect the man and the guts it took.

In the spring of 1990, **Carreras** had the idea of organizing a concert to celebrate the end of the Italia '90 World Cup. He knew that his buddies **Pavarotti** and **Domingo** were great football fans (what Americans call "soccer"), so he invited them to join him. On July 7, 1990, the Three Tenors sang at the Baths of Caracalla in Rome. The concert was televised all over the world. It became the best-selling opera video ever. It has spawned a few sequels and several pretty good operatic doo-wop groups.

ACT III:
LISTENING TO OPERA:
THE WAY IT'S REALLY DONE

RULE #1: IGNORE THE CONVENTIONAL ADVICE ON LISTENING TO OPERA

The usual bookish advice on listening to opera is unrealistic and pretty much guaranteed to chase people away from opera instead of drawing them into it. I know dozens of people who, like me, have become "converts" to opera after growing up listening to various kinds of popular music. We all began listening to opera in the same way. It's easy, it's fun and it's <u>natural</u>.

What IS the Conventional Advice?

The conventional advice is:

- Listen to the entire opera once or twice

- Read the entire libretto (ideally, as you listen to the opera)

- Go to the opera house and see the opera

That approach may eventually browbeat you into "appreciating" opera, but it kills any possibility of loving it. Most people didn't do that much homework at school, so they aren't likely to do it now.

Opera is a Madman's (or Madwoman's) Art.

**(If you approach it with too much sanity,
you miss the whole point of it!)**

Q: How do people really get started listening to opera?

A: It's the same way you get started listening to "normal" music when you don't have anybody standing over you with a stick: you listen to SINGERS– not composers–and you judge the singers the same way you judge singers in regular music: from your senses, your taste, your soul.

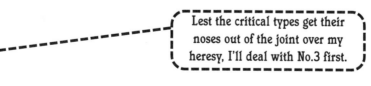

YOUR taste, not some critic's!

You listen to songs—or arias— not entire operas. Then, when the spirit strikes you, you listen to duets and trios and longer excerpts. It may be months (or years) before you listen to an entire opera. You do it when it seems natural—when you feel like doing it—not when someone says you should do it.

Opera is music, not medicine.

You begin by listening primarily to singers' opera. In the beginning, more often than not, that will be largely Italian opera—or "Italianate" opera—music in which the singers' approach is to sing beautifully and melodically regardless of the language. (I hear the music police banging on my door!)

... then compare, compare, compare ...

> Lest the critical types get their noses out of the joint over my heresy, I'll deal with No.3 first.

Listen to ITALIAN opera, not German

On the surface, the quote below merely records the first appearance in English of the Italian term "Bel Canto" ...

The Oxford English Dictionary gives the date of its first appearance in English as 1908, citing an article in the New York Daily Chronicle about the complaints of music critics that "audiences do not want Wagner" and that "the public flocks to the Italian Bel Canto."

—Henry Pleasants, The Great Singers (my emphasis)

Just beneath the surface, three points are made:

1. General audiences do NOT want Wagner

2. General audiences DO Want Italian Bel Canto

3. Those two facts "elicit the complaints"—*irritate the hell out of*—music critics.

THEREFORE RULE #2 IS ...

IGNORE THE CRITICS

A critic is a guy who makes a living looking down on things. Some generous people do it for free. Their entire personality consists of looking down their noses at everything!

> I criticize, therefore I am!

They play it safe. I am the opposite ...

> **"I'm a true adorer of life, and if I can't reach as high as the face of it, I plant my kiss somewhere further down"**
>
> –Saul Bellow, *Henderson the Rain King*

Cheap thrills, expensive thrills—I'll take them all. Critics can complain all they like, but that won't change the fact that virtually every new listener to opera, listens primarily to the <u>singing</u>. And anyone who listens to opera for the singing, listens primarily to Italian—or "Italianate" opera.

It really is (almost) that simple.

(Sorry, this is real life—everything has an almost in it.)

Of course there are German, French, (et cetera) singers and operas that should be included in any survey of opera—they are too beautiful to ignore! But if you want a rule for beginning listeners that holds true 90% of the time, it's simple: pay attention to what the critics say, and do the opposite! When it comes to opera, it's as if the critics have decided that ecstasy is a danger that must be stamped out at any cost.

There's a story they tell about Verdi ...

A Great Critic visited **Verdi** as he was putting the finishing touches on *Il Trovatore*.

"What do you think of this," Verdi asked him, playing the Anvil Chorus.

"Trash," announced the Great Critic, for he loved only the finest things.

"Now try this," said Verdi, offering the Miserere.

"What rubbish!" the Great Critic observed, for his nuanced sensibility could accept only the most profound art.

"One last test," said Verdi. He presented the tenor's aria, "Di quella pira."

"It's beastly" said the Critic, for anything less than nobility made him shudder.

Verdi rose from the piano and embraced the Great Critic in momentous joy.

"What is the meaning of this?" said the Great Critic.

"My dear friend," Verdi told him. "I have been writing a popular opera-an opera for the public, not for the purists and classicists and solemn judges like you. If you liked this music, no one else would. But your distaste assures me of success. In three months *Il Trovatore* will be sung, whistled and played all over Italy!"

—Ethan Mordden, *Opera Anecdotes*

Q: HOW DO REAL PEOPLE GET STARTED LISTENING TO OPERA?

A: *THEY FOCUS ON SINGERS.*

Q: BUT, BUT, BUT ... OPERA SINGERS ARE SO DIFFERENT THAN 'NORMAL' SINGERS?

NOT as different as you think.

Believe it or not, opera has a good deal in common with the music you already listen to. Many popular singers have/had "operatic" styles. Any singer who really belts out a song or who has conspicuously great high notes is getting very close to operatic. Any singer who sings with great emotional intensity is getting very close to operatic. The singing of a country's National Anthem is often an operatic endeavor—*(I want to sing so high and so loud and with such heroic intensity that I lift you right out of your seats!)*

Perfect Example: Whitney Houston's 1991 singing of the U.S. national anthem is considered by many (myself included) to be the best version of the National Anthem ever recorded. It became a top ten best seller—twice!—and was among Houston's best selling recordings.

It's only a couple minutes long and you can listen to it in 20 seconds. Simply:

Go to Google.

Type in: **whitney houston national anthem 1991**

Select the option that says "**YouTube**."

And listen to it! (It's only two minutes long.)

It's that simple!

You may object that some of the best versions of national anthems, including Houston's, are pretty radically improvised—*but so are opera arias!* That improvisation is what opera singers call "Fioratura."

Speaking of Similarities ... ?

If Smoky Robinson were an opera singer, he would be a smooth, beautiful-voiced, used-baloney salesman ... kind of like Beniamino Gigli—enraptured by his own bulljive. ("Ooo eee ooo, baby, baby ... How do you say that in Italian?) The similarity in singing styles between specific opera singers and "real" singers (Smokey and Beniamino Gigli!?!) might even be a good place for a new listener to start!

Although their voices were nothing alike, Billie Holiday and Maria Callas were two of a kind in a way that transcends music, from their breathtaking musical intelligence to their self-negating private lives.

(At the risk of sounding completely nuts, I almost believe that there was some kind of spiritual connection between those two brilliant black and white Athenas.)

Satchmo's hanky and Pavarotti's hanky? Damned if I know. (Jung's theory of Parallel Hankies?) The Gods of Music work in mysterious ways. Check this out ...

> **"I'm playin' a date in Florida, livin' in the colored section and I'm playin' my horn for myself one afternoon. A knock come on the door and there's an old, gray-haired flute player from the Philadelphia Orchestra, down there for his health. Walking through that neighborhood, he heard this horn, playing Cavalleria Rusticana, which he said he never heard phrased like that before."**
>
> — Louis Armstrong

To make the jump from (listening to) "regular" singers to opera singers, all you need is something to ignite a little spark.

How Do I Ignite the SPARK?

It's usually a particular singer that ignites the spark, but it could be a melody from a movie or TV. As I mentioned at the beginning of the book, one operatic piece that got a lot of love from normal people was the elegant duet in the movie *The Shawshank Redemption*. That duet, from Mozart's ***Le Nozze di Figaro*** (*The Marriage of Figaro*), was sung by **Gundula Janowitz** and **Edith Mathis**.

One Way That Real People
Expand Their Listening Options

If, for example, you found that duet quite beautiful and you reacted to it as you would if it were regular music, you might "Google it," find the duet on YouTube, listen to it and check out a different version of the same duet. YouTube offers several. I listened to a different version of the same duet, the one with **Gundula Janowitz** and **Lucia Popp**—two absolutely beautiful singers.

If **Lucia Popp** (the lighter-voiced singer) sounds good to you, you might want to listen to her version of other arias—perhaps the two spectacular "**Queen of the Night**" arias from Mozart's ***Magic Flute*** ...

Or if **Gundula Janowitz** gets your juices flowing, you can slide into a half hour of pure ecstasy by listening to her sing Strauss' **Four Last Songs** ...

(... and if you get off by catching people in foolish contradictions, you might enjoy bringing to my attention the facts that Mozart and Strauss are both German composers and Janowitz and Popp both specialize in German Opera ...)

(... to which I might reply—if I spoke my soul's truth—that they were so beautiful they transcended language and ethnicity. Call them anything you like, *just listen to them*.)

Challenging the Limits of Human Excellence

For what it's worth, athletes are often attracted to opera, partly because of the strength, skill and presence of mind involved in challenging the limits of human excellence and delivering a peak performance on demand.

> **THE LIMITS OF HUMAN EXCELLENCE**
> Olympic athletes have to deliver a peak performance every four years. Opera singers have to deliver a peak performance every four DAYS! Pavarotti had to hit those nine high Cs every four days! The mental and physical demands made on opera singers are almost impossible.

Athletes are also drawn to opera because they have heroic dreams. If you've downsized your dreams until they're invisible, opera is a good place to get them back.

Opera is heroic music.

("*Vincero! Vincero!*" Victory, in any language, any sport, any life situation ...)

OTHER WAYS TO IGNITE THE SPARK:

ETHNICITY and Well-Padded Role Models

Seeing yourself in one of the performers can ignite the Spark.

If you're not exactly the skinny type, it's kind of wonderful to see all those well-padded people being admired, adored and celebrated. If you are seriously ethnic (or God forbid, a minority), seeing someone from your ethnic group loved, admired, respected, can light your fire ...

PAUL ROBESON, born in Princeton New Jersey in 1898, was an honor student at Rutgers University, a two-time football All-American, graduated from Columbia Law school, played in an NFL Championship football game, was a professional stage actor and a fine opera and concert singer.

In 1928 he moved to England, then returned to sing a sold-out concert at Carnegie Hall. He specialized in black folk music and songs from Italian and German opera and he spoke 20 languages. In 1934 he visited the Soviet Union. In 1948 he attended the World Peace Congress. In 1959 he gave his final performance of Othello. He died in 1976. He often said, **"I must feed the people with my songs."**

SPARK, HELL! ROBESON LIVED A LIFE SO FULL IT COULD IGNITE A BOMB!

If there ever was a Role Model worth emulating, it's Paul Robeson.

MEANWHILE BACK AT THE OPERA HOUSE ...

ETHNIC DIVERSITY

Major opera houses are like ethnic Noah's Arks: they have a couple of everything. It is not unusual to see an opera featuring a Spanish tenor, an African-American soprano, a Polish mezzo, a Puerto Rican baritone, a bass from Nebraska and a Jewish conductor. The Metropolitan Opera roster includes Japanese, Chinese and Korean singers who specialize in Italian opera!

Other things can ignite the Spark: movies or boredom or the irrepressible impulse to capitalize words like Passion, Romance, Destiny—even though in real life they may be extremely lower-case.

But make no mistake about it—80% of the time, the Spark is lit by a singer. An opera singer.

It starts with one particular singer. All you have to do is find him, her, it, or them.

Two Singers Who Have Ignited the SPARK
in Millions of People

The first, **Luciano Pavarotti**, is so obvious it's a No-Brainer. I wouldn't be surprised if Pavarotti brought more new listeners to opera than all other modern opera singers combined. It is fashionable at the moment to knock Pavarotti (there is no snob value in loving Pavarotti) but he was a magnificent tenor with a career spanning some forty years. His voice (like every other singer) was fresher and more energetic during the earlier part of his career. The early recordings of singers like Pavarotti and Bjorling overflow with irrepressible energy. Not only are the recordings more accessible today than they were during the singers' lifetimes but, counter-intuitive as it may seem, old recordings are getting better all the time. (See the APPENDIX on how Stefan Zucker restores old, scratchy recordings and videos.)

The second singer who has brought millions of listeners toward opera (but has left most of them reluctant to go all the way) is **Andrea Bocelli**. At the risk of riling Bocelli's rabid fans, I would describe Bocelli's voice, at its best, as a sort of Pavarotti-Lite. Like Pavarotti, Bocelli's voice is/was beautiful, utterly "Italianate"—smooth, romantic, flowing *legato*. Bocelli's singing of hybrid "popera" is quite wonderful (especially "*Il mare calmo della sera*")—and I like the fact that he has the courage to try opera. Unfortunately, most of his fans refuse to see his (obvious to us) limitations as an opera singer.

... and in a sort of parallel universe of intolerance, most opera fans are too uppity to enjoy Bocelli!

Opera lovers and haters alike, Google & YouTube Bocelli singing "*Il mare calmo della sera*."

It's really good. A word to Bocelli fans: Bocelli has given you an idiot-proof intro to REAL opera. Come all the way into opera instead of resenting the fact that most opera listeners don't consider Bocelli a great opera singer. You don't have to choose between Bocelli and Bjorling or Pavarotti or Florez or Domingo or Joseph Schmidt or Lauritz Melchoir or Lawrence Brownlee.

When you are given a choice between two—or two dozen—wonderful *anythings*—**take ALL of 'em**!

SCENE 16: IN SEARCH OF MIRACULOUS SINGERS

If I had to name three singers who would be most likely to bliss you out, have you kissing snakes on the forehead and send shivers up your spine, I'd say **Jussi Bjorling**, **Leontyne Price** and young **Ezio Pinza**.

Jussi Bjorling

Bjorling is the guy who "introduced" me to opera. It went like this, I was in the Army, a 19-year-old rhythm-and-blues Detroit kid, all libido and no brains, sentenced to six months in Alabama, when one day a friend I didn't particularly like came up to me, drunk as an upright man can be, and in a tone you'd used to confess that you molested nuns, whispered, *"I'm studying Opera."* He begged me to listen to a record with him—"I have to share this with somebody." Even at 19, I was supportive of friends even if I didn't particularly like them, so I tried (*pretended?*) to be broad-minded. He put on the record; I sat in a dark corner so he couldn't read my face; he said it was a guy named **Jussi Bjorling**; he thanked me; he sat down; he shut up.

BAM! BONK! BOINK!!!

I'm not a very holy guy—I've never had a certifiable religious experience—but, at 19, that was as close as I'd come. I had never heard anything so miraculous in my life. Clarity, power, beauty, focus—the *Sound* of the Heroic! (Whatever in the hell that means?) There was no getting used to it, no studying books or librettos, no intention to "appreciate" anything. (I was a teenager—I already <u>knew</u> everything). In a flash, like Saint What's-His-Name getting knocked off his pony, I was an instant convert. One of Plato's most off-the-wall ideas is that we have the knowledge of nearly everything already inside us; all we need is a guy like Socrates to ask us the right questions or a drunk to play a record that will teach us what we already know ...

There was no learning, no transition, no anything! I heard the voice, and BAM! It was as if there was a door locked inside of me that I was unaware of, and this Voice unlocks it.

The door opens; I open; everything opens.

... and I'm not the person I was.

Leontyne Price

If I had to choose the single-most electrifying voice I ever heard on anybody, anywhere, ever, it would be the Voice of **Leontyne Price** (b. 1927). Price's voice is rich, opulent, thrilling. If any Voice could slap you in the head and throw you up against the wall, it would be **Leontyne's**.

IF YOU WANT A TASTE OF WHAT I'M TALKING ABOUT

In Act Two of Verdi's Ernani, Leontyne Price's electrifying voice comes zinging in out of left field again and again. Lyric tenor Carlo Bergonzi sounds ok but he sounds a bit bland and underpowered next to Leontyne.

(Google & YouTube it if you want to sample it)

With both **Bjorling** and **Price**, you'll find a range of recordings some 30 years apart. My suggestion is get them when they were young. At a later age, both singers will have developed more finesse, but finesse is a bridesmaid's art. I want you to hear the Voice in all its beautiful brainless glory.

Ezio Pinza

After not hearing the Voice of the young **Pinza** (1892-1957) for a few months, I will play one of his recordings from the 1930s. (In one of my minds, I stagger backward, I clutch my chest, I mutter, *"I'm, coming, Elizabeth."*) Pinza's voice is so magnificent that it's hard to hold in the mind—truly one of the Voices of God.

However: Pinza's voice had a "window" of magnificence. In his early years (the 1920s), he had such a fast vibrato that it tended to obscure the beauty of his voice. In later years (after 1940), his voice sounded much more common (merely VERY good instead of miraculous).

If you listen to a recording of **Pinza** from the 1930s, you will understand why people like me turn into sanctified maniacs over opera.

50 of the Greatest Singers who ever lived

After **Bjorling**, **Price** and **Pinza**, which singers are most likely to grab you by the ears and demand your attention? Like many opera fanatics, I am a bit partial to tenors, so I will give you MY quick list of all-time great singers (primarily in the past). In no particular order, broken into categories (by the type of opera they sing), here are (in my opinion) 50 of the greatest singers who have ever lived:

ITALIAN TENORS	GERMAN TENORS
JUSSI BJORLING	LAURITZ MELCHOIR
LUCIANO PAVAROTTI	HELGE ROSWAENGE
ENRICO CARUSO	MARCEL WITTRISCH
BENIAMINO GIGLI	FRITZ WUNDERLICH
GIUSEPPE DI STEFANO	JULIUS PATZAK
MARIO DEL MONACO	SIEGFRIED JERUSALEM
PLACIDO DOMINGO	RICHARD TAUBER
ANTONIO CORTIS	JOSEPH SCHMIDT
JOSEPH CALLEJA	WOLFGANG WINDGASSEN
GIUSEPPE MORINO	REINER GOLDBERG

SOPRANOS

MARIA CALLAS

LEONTYNE PRICE

RITA STREICH

FRIDA LEIDER

GUNDULA JANOWITZ

JESSYE NORMAN

ELISABETH RETHBERG

LEYLA GENCER

RENEE FLEMING

MAGDA OLIVERO

MEZZOS & CONTRALTOS

EWA PODLES

MARILYN HORNE

CECILIA BARTOLI

VESSELINA KASAROVA

MAHALIA JACKSON

ORALIA DOMINGUEZ

KATHLEEN FERRIER

MAUREEN FORRESTER

CONCHITA SUPERVIA

FREDERICA VON STADE

BARITONES

ETTORE BASTIANINI

TITO GOBBI

PAVEL LISITSIAN

GIORGIO ZANCANERO

VLADIMIR CHERNOV

TITTA RUFFO

BASS & BASS-BARITONE

BORIS CHRISTOFF

EZIO PINZA

KURT MOLL

SAMUEL RAMEY

DMITRI HVOROSTOVSKY

BRYN TERFEL

In real life, opera fans do not spend the majority of their listening time at the opera house. Most of our listening is done at home or during some other everyday activity. We listen primarily to great singers. Odd as it may sound, listening helps us clarify our taste. Do you prefer tenors or sopranos or like both equally? Do you like high voices or low? Intense emotion or mellow and restrained?

More about that as we go.

If singers are the most important variable in opera, how do we know the good singers from the bad?

The list of singers above are great singers from the past, so I chose them according to my own taste.

The singers you will see—if you're lucky—are the best singers in the world right now. Instead of confining them to my taste, I have looked for the singers that most opera-goers consider currently the best singers in the world. (from Operatoonity.com—silly name, but good list)

Best Male Opera Singers in the World Now

Roberto Alagna, French tenor

Marcelo Alvarez, Argentine lyric tenor

Lawrence Brownlee, American tenor

Joseph Calleja, Maltese tenor

Carlo Colombara, Italian bass

Placido Domingo, Spanish tenor and conductor

Gerald Finley, Canadian bass-baritone

Juan Diego Florez, Peruvian tenor

Ferrucio Furlanetto, Italian bass

Vittorio Grigolo, Italian tenor

Thomas Hampson, American baritone

Dmitri Hvorostovsky, Russian baritone

Jonas Kaufmann, German spinto tenor

Simon Keenlyside, British baritone

Mariusz Kwiecien, Polish baritone

James Morris, American bass-baritone

Rene Pape, German bass

Ruggero Raimondi, Italian bass-baritone

Erwin Schrott, Uruguayan bass-baritone

Stuart Skelton, Australian heldentenor

Bryn Terfel, Welsh bass-baritone

John Tomlinson, English bass

Ramon Vargas, Mexican tenor

Personally, I would add two singers:

Rolando Villazon, Mexican lyric tenor

Stephen Costello, American lyric tenor

Best Female Opera Singers in the World Now

Cecilia Bartoli, Italian mezzo-soprano
Olga Borodina, Russian mezzo-soprano
Sarah Connolly, British mezzo-soprano
Fiorenza Cedolins, Italian soprano
Diana Damrau, German lyric coloratura soprano
Annette Dasch, German soprano
Natalie Dessay, French coloratura soprano
Mariella Devia, Italian soprano
Joyce DiDonato, American mezzo soprano
Renee Fleming, American soprano
Angela Gheorghiu, Romanian soprano
Anja Harteros, German soprano
Magdelena Kozena, Czech mezzo-soprano
Aleksandra Kurzak, Polish coloratura soprano
Waltraud Meier, German dramatic soprano
Anna Netrebko, Russian soprano
Patricia Racette, American soprano
Sondra Radvanovsky, American soprano
Dorothea Roschmann, German soprano
Rinat Shaham, Israeli mezzo soprano
Nina Stemme, Swedish soprano
Anne Sofie von Otter, Swedish mezzo soprano

Q: How important are the singers in a live performance of an opera?

A: That's easy. SINGERS are the most important part of opera. Most opera nuts are fussier about singers than we are about the food we eat or the clothes we wear. Most of us would throw away a ticket to an opera with lousy singers.

117

Q: How can I know in advance if a particular singer is good or bad?

A: Google any singer by name. You'll see a list of reviews, articles, Wikipedia, etc. But the only test that matters is how the singer sounds to YOU. Listen to him/her on YouTube or find a free MP3 recording (Google) or a CD for sale on Amazon and listen to the 30-60 second samples. (You can tell in 20 seconds if you love or hate a Voice!) YOU are the ONLY judge that matters. If you love the singer, zoom to the opera immediately. If you don't ... why bother?

The ultimate decision of whether a particular singer is good or not is YOURS. Don't waste your time listening to lousy singers. Be honest with yourself.

LISTENING TO WAGNER
Many People Are Intimidated by Wagner.
(He'd love that!)

Q: Is there a painless way to get started listening to his music?

A: Yes, but it's different than with other composers. With other opera composers, you find your way in through singers. With Wagner, you find your way in through his orchestral music. Pick up one of those CDs/DVDs/YouTube selections with names like "Orchestral Selections from Wagner's Ring." (If there's nothing on there that grabs your attention... call a doctor.) A few of the obvious choices are:

- The Entrance of the Gods into Valhalla
- The Ride of the Valkyries
- Siegfried's Rhine Journey
- Siegfried's Funeral March

Don't even think of saying you don't like Wagner. There's so much variety in his music that, if you don't like one piece, you're bound to love another. And if that doesn't work—or even if it does—there is a hilarious and educational monologue by **Anna Russell**, a British lady, on Wagner's Ring. It's brilliant.

ACT FOUR:
LISTENER-FRIENDLY OPERAS

Aida	Verdi	Italian	1871	Late Verdi
Barber of Seville	Rossini	Italian	1816	Bel Canto-comic
Bluebeard's Castle	Bartok	Hungarian	1918	Modern Allegorical
La Boheme	Puccini	Italian	1896	Romantic/Verismo
Boris Godunov	Mussorgsky	Russian	1874	Russian Historical
Carmen	Bizet	French	1875	French Verismo
Cavalleria Rusticana	Mascagni	Italian	1890	Italian Verismo
Don Giovanni	Mozart	Ital.(Ger.)	1787	Opera Buffa
Elixir of Love	Donizetti	Italian	1832	Bel Canto-comic
Faust	Gounod	French	1859	French Romantic
Fledermaus	Strauss, J.	German	1874	German Operetta
Les Huguenots	Meyerbeer	French	1836	French Grand Opera
Lucia di Lammermoor	Donizetti	Italian	1835	Bel Canto-serious
Madame Butterfly	Puccini	Italian	1904	Romantic/Versimo
Magic Flute	Mozart	German	1791	German Singspeil
Manon	Massenet	French	1884	French Romantic
Norma	Bellini	Italian	1831	Bel Canto-serious
Pagliacci	Leoncavallo	Italian	1892	Italian Verismo
Peter Grimes	Britten	British	1945	Modern British
Porgy and Bess	Gershwin	American	1935	American
Rigoletto	Verdi	Italian	1851	Early Verdi
Rosenkavalier	Strauss, R.	German	1911	NeoClassic Parody
Tales of Hoffman	Offenbach	French	1881	Romantic Allegory
Tosca	Puccini	Italian	1900	Romantic/Verismo
La Traviata	Verdi	Italian	1853	Middle Verdi
Il Trovatore	Verdi	Italian	1853	Middle Verdi
Rheingold	Wagner	German	1869	The Ring Cycle, 1
Die Walkure	Wagner	German	1870	The Ring Cycle, 2
Siegfried	Wagner	German	1876	The Ring Cycle, 3
Gotterdammerung	Wagner	German	1876	The Ring Cycle, 4

TWO QUESTIONS

Q: How can I understand opera if I don't understand the language it's sung in?

A: Some years ago, on a moonlit night in Central Park, my wife and I saw classical actress Gloria Foster play Clytemnestra in the old Greek drama Agamemnon. Foster was awesome. In a climactic scene, she didn't use a word of English or any other dictionary language. She used her body and her soul and syllables and sounds and she conveyed the most profound sense of anguish I've ever seen outside of real life. You couldn't misunderstand it even if you wanted to.

Point 1: Trust yourself—go with your feelings—you'll understand.

Point 2: Most opera plots make better sense if you don't understand the language. Like the man says ...

> **I am ravaged by opera, on condition that I have only a vague idea of what it is about.** —James Agate [1877-1947]

Or, if you prefer

> **"Opera in English ... is just about as sensible as baseball in Italian."** — H.L. Mencken

Point 3: I have made the assumption here that you aren't going to rush out and learn Italian, German, etc.; if opera does entice you to learn a language or two, you can thank me later.

Q: On what basis did you choose the operas? The most listener-friendly? The most popular? Most important? Personal favorites?

A: If I chose the most popular operas, you'd have two French operas (*Carmen* and *Faust*), one German (*Magic Flute*), and the rest Italian (*Cav* and *Pag*, a few **Bel Canto** operas, and everything ever written by **Verdi** and **Puccini**).

If I chose <u>my</u> favorites, we'd have a **Rossini** festival, lots of **Bellini** and **Donizetti**, Beethoven's *Fidelio*, a couple of French tearjerkers (*Werther*, *Romeo Et Juliet*), a few oddities (*La Fiamma, Guntram*), a drastically condensed version of Wagner's *Ring* and we'd omit *Porgy*, *Carmen*, and probably *Don Giovanni*, and trade the Verdi, Puccini, and Strauss operas in for their less famous counterparts (*Salome, Fanciulla del West, Manon Lescaut, Forza del Destino, Don Carlos, Sicilian Vespers.*)

If I chose most important, we have snorers like **Gluck** and **Schoenberg**, more **Wagner**, **Monteverdi**.

I chose the operas based on these criteria:

1. First and foremost, they had to be listener friendly—something you could really enjoy listening to.

2. The second criterion: they had to be as varied as possible, both linguistically and stylistically. The operas I've chosen cover seven different languages (as any fool knows, English is one language, American is another). Stylistically, they cover high and low Mozart, funny and serious Bel Canto, a 20-year span of Verdi, plus French and Italian Verismo, French Grand Opera, Russian opera, French Tear Jerker, German operetta, French operetta gone highbrow, Hungarian allegorical opera, German neoclassical, modern British, Jazzified American, along with Puccini and Wagner—each a class unto himself.

3. Wagner's Ring Cycle had to get in.

4. When I had any wiggle room, I chose the ones I loved.

HERE THEY ARE.
I HOPE YOU LOVE' EM...

AIDA

GIUSEPPE VERDI

BOTTOM LINE: It's a love story between an Ethiopian slave girl, Aida, and a captain in the Egyptian army, Radames.

ACT 1:

Radames wants to become a general in the Egyptian army and marry Aida—but Amneris, the Egyptian king's daughter, is hot for Radames' body.

ACT 2:

Radames and the Egyptian army return triumphantly from war ... with Aida's father (the King of Ethiopia) in captivity.

ACT 3:

Aida sweet-talks Radames into betraying the Egyptian army. Radames does it, then overcome by guilt, he surrenders to the Egyptian priests.

ACT 4:

The priests punish Radames by burying him alive in a tomb. Princess Amneris weeps melodically at the tomb's entrance. Aida, who has been hiding voluptuously in the tomb, reveals herself to Radames so they sing a love duet ... and die together.

BARBER OF SEVILLE
GIOACCHINO ROSSINI

BOTTOM LINE: It's a comedy about a count and his girl trying to get married, assisted by the town barber (and busybody), and obstructed by everyone else.

ACT I:
Count Almaviva serenades Rosina, but her guardian Dr. Bartolo won't let her see Almaviva because the old lech Bartolo wants her for himself.

The Barber and the Count hatch a plot whereby the Count disguises himself as a drunk soldier assigned to live in Dr. Bartolo's house. Disruption ensues and the coppers arrive.

ACT 2:
The Count comes to Bartolo's house newly disguised as a professor to sit in for Rosina's "sick" music teacher. The Count, with the Barber's help, overcomes all the bad guys and marries Rosina.

COMPARE: Giovanni Paisiello (1740-1816) wrote an earlier version of The Barber of Seville (1782).

BLUEBEARD'S CASTLE
BELA BARTOK

BOTTOM LINE: A moody masterpiece with a powerful identity. Part universal mythology, part Freudian allegory ... and maybe the only Hungarian opera you'll ever hear.

ACT I:

Bluebeard, a cross between Don Juan and Dracula, "interviews" Judith to see if she'll become his wife. He points to seven doors flanking the hall of his castle. Through the first door, a torture chamber is revealed. The second door is hung with Bluebeard's weaponry. One by one the doors are opened, each worse than the one before. ("Sorrow, Judith. Sorrow," is the way Bluebeard describes his Lake of Tears.)

Bluebeard opens the last locked door only after Judith's insistence. One by one, Bluebeard's wives file out. "Living, living..." Judith says incredulously. Then she joins Bluebeard's parade of living-dead wives ...

It's a one-act opera with two characters. Balsy, experimental, and wonderful. It has such a strong musical identity that if you hear two chords you know it's *Bluebeard's Castle*.

"Similar stories appear in European, African, and Eastern folklore; the essentials are the murderous husband, the locked, forbidden room, and the wife's curiosity."   —Encyclopedia Britannica

125

LA BOHEME
GIACOMO PUCCINI

BOTTOM LINE: Poor, struggling artists–"Bohemians"–in 1800s Paris fall madly, melodically in love.

ACT I:

Rodolfo the poet, Marcello the painter, Colline the philosopher, and Schaunard the musician outslick their landlord, who has come to collect the rent. Rodolfo the poet meets Mimi the seamstress and they fall head over heels.

ACT 2:

At the Café Momus, Marcello the painter sees his old girlfriend, Musetta the tart, who sings a famous waltz and sends him on a jive errand.

ACT 3:

Outside an inn on the outskirts of Paris, Rodolfo and Mimi decide they can't hack it together and, in an outpouring of melody, break up.

ACT 4:

Mimi is dying; Musetta, the tart with a heart of gold, sells her earrings to buy medicine; Rodolfo shows up just past the nick of time; Mimi melodically bites the dust. Rodolfo (Caruso, Gigli, Bjoerling, di Stefano, Pavarotti) screams her name—"Mimi! Mimi!"—and even if you're laughing, sends chills through you.

COMPARE: Leoncavallo (composer of *Pagliacci*) also wrote a decent version of *La Boheme*. The aria "Testa adorata" (Caruso, Gigli, Franco Bonisolli, Mario Lanza) is the most hysterically over the top aria ever. Enjoy!!

BORIS GODUNOV
MODEST MUSSORGSKY

BOTTOM LINE: Monkey business in 17th-century Russia

PROLOGUE:

When the Russian Czar Ivan the Terrible died in 1584, one of his sons was a child and the other was a teenage halfwit, so Boris Godunov, the Czar's advisor, became acting Czar. The small child, Dimitri, died in a monastery and the feebleminded brother died not long after. In Scene 2, Boris, the newly crowned Czar, is having trouble with his conscience because he ordered the murder of the little boy.

ACT I:

Five years later, an opportunistic novice monk who is the same age the dead Dimitri would have been, decides to pretend that he himself is Prince Dimitri.

ACT 2:

Boris, in a great monologue, laments that things are going badly in Russia and everyone blames the Czar. His advisor Prince Shuiski warns Boris that a pretender after the throne is winning the people to his side. Boris asked Shuiski if he's certain that it was little Dimitri who was killed. Shuiski leaves; Boris imagines that he sees the bloodstained body of the murdered boy and begs God for forgiveness.

ACTS 3 & 4:

The false Dmitri promises to rid the people of Boris; they follow him.

An old monk tells Boris of a shepherd's dream about the murder of Dimitri. Boris, gasping for air, sends for his son Feodor. Boris sings an incredibly moving farewell to little Feodor, then dies gloriously.

Check out an astonishing five-minute video on YouTube in which Bulgarian Basso Boris Christoff saunters into a recording studio in 'civilian clothes' (sweater vest & tie), greets everyone casually, and with no fuss whatsoever, records a heartbreaking scene from the opera. Amazing!

CARMEN
GEORGES BIZET

BOTTOM LINE: A love story between a sexy, manipulative Gypsy girl (Carmen) and a naïve soldier (Don Jose) who's just dyin' to be made a fool of.

ACT I:

In Spain: Don Jose arrests Carmen for causing a disturbance. She gives him a big smile and a little feel and he lets her escape ... for which he is arrested.

ACT 2:

At an inn: Carmen meets the disgraced Jose after he is released from jail, gives him a big smile and a little feel, and talks him into joining her band of smugglers.

ACT 3:

Meanwhile: Micaela, Don Jose's old squeeze, comes looking for him to tell him that his mother is dying. Don Jose goes to see his dying mother.

ACT 4:

Meanwhile: Carmen becomes the lover of a bullfighter (probably just to shut him up so he'll stop singing that damned "Toreador" song). Jealous Don Jose—no big surprise!—loses his cool, sings some dynamite high notes, and kills Carmen.

YouTube Gem: Recording the last scene of Carmen, Super-Soprano Jessye Norman looks on in astonishment as journeyman tenor Neil Shicoff pours every bit of his soul into his role as Don Jose.

CAVALLERIA RUSTICANA
PIETRO MASCAGNI

BOTTOM LINE: A story of jealousy, love, and death. (a.k.a., an average day in Sicily)

ACT 1:

Easter Sunday, Town Square, Sicily: Santuzza—the nice girl—is worried that her hotblooded fiancé Turiddu is having an affair with the hotblooded Lola who was once Turiddu's ol' lady but is now married to Alfio the hotblooded Teamster. (Sicily? Alfio the Teamster? You could finish the damn thing yourself!)

Outside the church: Santuzza tries crying to Mama Lucia (Turridu's mother—a saint), but Mama doesn't want to hear it.

Santuzza goes whining to Turiddu, appealing to his sense of fair play and justice. Turiddu knocks her to the ground. Santuzza, really pissed now, tells Lola's husband, Alfio the teamster. ("*MaaRONE!*")
   Alfio the Teamster challenges Turiddu to a duel. Turiddu gets drunk and barely finishes singing good bye to his hotblooded mother before Alfio the hotblooded Teamster kills him.

YouTube has a video of the great Beniamino Gigli singing CAV with his feet (and sometimes the top of his head) cut off! A truly beautiful voice coming from a transcendent Bullshit Artist!

Opera at its campy best.

 + +

JUST ANOTHER DAY IN SICILY.

DON GIOVANNI
WOLFGANG A. MOZART

BOTTOM LINE: Don (Juan) Giovanni, the great lover, gets what he deserves.

ACT 1:

With the help of his servant Leporello, Don puts a move on Anna, kills her father, gets away from her boyfriend Ottavio, runs into an old girlfriend (Elvira), and leaves Leporello behind to "explain." Don runs across a pretty young thang (Zerlina) and invites her to his castle. Act 1 ends as Zerlina run screaming in pantyhose terror and the Don is cornered by all of his enemies at once. Don may be a lech, but he's no coward: he swashbuckles his way to freedom.

ACT 2:

The randy Don trades clothes with Leporello with the intent of hitting on Elvira's maid but ends up outsmarting himself: Elvira sees Leporello dressed in the Don's clothing, and runs off with Leporello. (Mozart wrote a "low comedy" scene that comes next, but most productions omit it because it doesn't fit with Mozart's lofty reputation.) As a joke, Don invites a statue of Anna's dead father to dinner. The statue actually comes and Don and his palace disappear in flames. Sometimes the opera ends there; sometimes it ends the way Mozart wrote it: with a goofy finale in which everyone tells us their plans—both young couples will be married, Leporello finds a nice dull master, and Elvira enters a convent.

(Maybe that's why Pope What's-His-Name had that opera house burned down; maybe he got sick of all those deranged opera ladies running off to convents.)

ELIXIR OF LOVE
GAETANO DONIZETTI

BOTTOM LINE: Comedy about a phony love potion sold by a quack ... but it ultimately works.

ACT 1:

Adina, wealthy, is loved, admired, and lusted after by both Sgt. Belcore and Nemorino, a shy but dumb peasant. Nemorino is conned by Dr. Dulcamara, the "medicine man" (in a duet as full of surprise and life as a magician's hat, especially when Pavarotti rocks it) into spending all of his money for a Love Potion (wine) that is *guaranteed* to make Adina love him within 24 hours. Unfortunately, Adina promises to marry Sgt. Belcore that night.

ACT 2:

Nemorino, no dummy, comes up with a brilliant solution. He joins the friggin Army and uses his enlistment money to buy a Magic Potion (wine) that is *guaranteed* to work in a half hour. After he gets a little bombed, Nemorino (Caruso, Gigli, Bjoerling, Pavarotti and every tenor in the universe) sings *"Una furtiva lagrima.."* Adina falls madly in love with him, buys back his enlistment, and they ... be doop, be doop, bedoop.

POPERA: Sometimes popular singers have a go at opera arias. "Una furtiva lagrima" is one of the most popular. Some are pretty good. Michael Bolton's version is so painful it's interesting.

FAUST
CHARLES GOUNOD

BOTTOM LINE: An old philosopher sells his soul to the devil to be young & studly again.

ACT 1:

Faust (an old philosopher) makes a deal with Mephistopheles (the devil): on Earth, Faust will be the master; later, he will serve Mephistopheles. They go off together seeking adventure.

ACT 2:

Faust, young and handsome, romances Marguerite. (He romances her so well she becomes pregnant.)

ACT 3:

In church, Marguerite prays that her sins be pardoned. Her brother Valentin comes back from the war to avenge his sister's honor, sings one of the prettiest baritone arias in Grand Opry ... then gets killed by Faust.

ACT 4:

Marguerite is in prison for killing her child. She prays to God— God saves her. You're right, the story <u>does</u> sound unfinished. That's where the music comes in. The music finishes it. The music sends Marguerite, Faust, you, me, your old Volkswagen—all of us— straight up to ... give it whatever name you like.

COMPARE: Arrigio Boito (1842-1918), author of some of Verdi's best librettos, composed *Mefistofele* (1868), an opera that is as good or better than Gounoud's Faust.

X SIGN HERE

DIE FLEDERMAUS
JOHANN STRAUSS

BOTTOM LINE: the quintessential Strauss 'Operation'

"... Beverly Sills, who can sing everything from Verdi's ballads to Strauss operations."

—President Gerald Ford, introducing opera singer Beverly Sills at the White House, 1975.

As usual, the Prez got his verbals mixed up: the word he wanted was "operetta." (Operetta = spoken dialogue with arias, sometimes beautiful, sometimes so pretty they're cloying; it <u>always</u> has a happy ending.) The Strauss in question isn't *Richard*, it's *Johann*, the heavyweight champ of the welterweight art of German operetta. This one is so good that the Met features it on New Year's Eve.

ACT 1:
Alfredo, a former boyfriend—and an Italian tenor—serenades Rosalinde, Eisenstein's wife. Eisenstein is supposed to go to jail that night but instead he goes to a party. He'll go to jail tomorrow.

ACT 2:
The party is a masked ball thrown by Prince Orlofsky. Eisenstein doesn't recognize his own wife, who flirts with him and takes his watch.

ACT 3:
Eisenstein reports to jail the next morning, but he finds that Alfredo, who'd been at Eisenstein's house sniffing after Rosalinde, was mistaken for Eisenstein and taken to jail in his stead. (What it lacks in dramatic urgency, it makes up for in toe-tapping music.)

LES HUGUENOTS
GIACOMO MEYERBEER

BOTTOM LINE: Just because critics badmouth French Grand Opera doesn't mean you shouldn't check it out. This is the best of the bunch, but you will have difficulty seeing it performed because it requires seven masterful singers.

PRELUDE AND ACTS 1, 2, 3, 4 (and sometimes) 5:

The growing hostility between Catholics and Protestants (Huguenots) in 16th century France impels Queen Marguerite to find some way to unite them. To that end, she ask Raoul, a young Huguenot nobleman, to marry Valentine, the daughter of a prominent Catholic.

When Valentine shows herself, Raoul furiously backs out of the deal to marry her—because he's been led to believe that she is the mistress of his Catholic friend, Count de Nevers. By the time Raoul admits to himself that he's hopelessly crazy about Valentine, she's been promised to de Nevers (although she is madly in love with Raoul and has even saved his life).

Raoul, brain-dead with love, sneaks into Valentine's room to "bid her a final farewell," but when he hears her father and other Catholic leaders coming, he hides behind a curtain. To his horror, he hears them planning to massacre the Huguenots that very night, the eve of St. Bartholomew. He goes to warn his friends, but the massacre is already in full swing. Valentine joins him and dies in his arms.

There are lots of great recorded excerpts from *Les Huguenots*. One of the greatest is a recording of German tenor Marcel Wittrisch and soprano Margarete Teschemacher singing the Raul/Valentine duet. It has one of the greatest high notes in recorded opera.

LUCIA DI LAMMERMOOR
GAETANO DONIZETTI

BOTTOM LINE: Lucia's slippery brother forces her to marry a rich guy she doesn't love, so Lucia goes crazy and kills the rich guy.

ACT 1:

Enrico needs money and wants his sister Lucia to marry rich Arturo in a "marriage of convenience"—Enrico's convenience. Lucia is in love with Edgardo, a guy from the neighborhood (Caruso, Pavarotti, etc.) who saved her life.

ACT 2:

Lucia's slippery brother not only intercepts all the letters Edgardo sends her, but the slimeball even forges a letter saying that Edgardo has married another lady. Lucia, heartbroken, marries the rich dude.

ACT 3:

Lucia goes extremely crazy, stumbling around, singing music of impossible fanciness ... she kills her husband, then herself. Edgardo, her loverboy, hears about the tragedy, he kills himself.

NOTE: Although this is a juicy role for sopranos, they sort of hate it because after they die, the tenor has the last 15 minutes onstage all to himself.

MADAME BUTTERFLY
GIACOMO PUCCINI

BOTTOM LINE: A naïve 15-year-old Japanese girl marries an American sailor.

ACT 1:
Japan; a marriage broker arranges a union between Lieut. Pinkerton and Madame Butterfly (a.k.a. Cio-Cio San). Sharpless, the American consul, warns Pinkerton that he isn't taking the marriage seriously enough. Butterfly's family rejects her for marrying a foreigner.

ACT 2:
Japan: Pinkerton has been gone for three years. A Japanese man wants to marry Butterfly, but she tells him she's already married. She has a child whom she's nicknamed "Trouble."

ACT 3:
Japan: Pinkerton returns with his new American wife and learns that he has a son. The grief-stricken Butterfly kills herself.

GOOD, BAD & UGLY

- Butterfly's aria "Un bel dì" is the Mother of All Ravishing but Embarrassing Puccini Tear Jerkers.

- Tenor Lovers like me don't love operas in which the tenor evaporates after the First Act.

- Japan, Viet Nam, Iraq, Afghanistan ... this is not some cute melodic fantasy. It's too prosaically real for opera.

MAGIC FLUTE
WOLFGANG A. MOZART

BOTTOM LINE: Prince Tamino, with the help of his Magic Flute, rescues Princess Pamina.

ACT 1:

Prince Tamino is saved from a bad snake by three women who hang out with the fancy singing Queen of the night. Papageno, a bull-slinging bird catcher, takes credit for killing the snake, but the women punish him for being a jive turkey.

The Queen of the Night sends Tamino and Pa-Pa-Papageno to rescue her daughter Pamina from Sarastro. The big-hearted Queen gives a Tamino a magic flute and Papageno magic bells.

ACT 2:

Papageno and the Prince (formerly known as Tamino) face a series of tests from Sarastro. Tamino ends up with Pamina; Papageno ends up with a chick who had a full-body facelift named Papagena ... and amid thunder and lightning, they melodically overcome the forces of evil ... whoever they were?

Don't fret if you can't tell the Good Guys from the Bad Guys–no one else can either. The Prince & Princess are Good, so are PapagenOH and PapagenAH. Everyone else? The Queen of the Night, a Bi-Polar UberColoratura, is a Good Guy in her first mind-blowing aria and a Bad Guy in her second utterly impossible aria. Add a bunch of muddy Masonic folklore, then ignore all of it and enjoy the music.

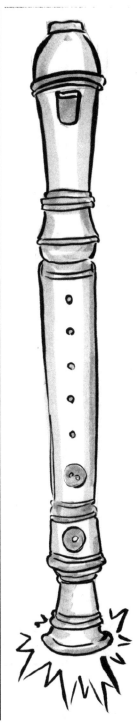

MANON
JULES MASSENET

BOTTOM LINE: An innocent, sheltered girl gives in to her craving for a life of luxury, excitement and love.

ACT 1:
On the way to the convent(!), Manon meets and falls in love with des Grieux. She skips the convent and splits to Paris with des Grieux.

ACT 2:
Manon and des Grieux are living happily ever after in Paris until des Grieux is somewhat kidnapped, after which de Bretigny (a filthy rich friend of Manon's slippery brother Lescaut) wins Manon's heart, mind and body with expensive crap.

ACT 3:
Des Grieux is so bummed out he decides to become a priest. Manon finds out, goes and rubs her nice little body up against him; he decides he isn't cut out for the priesthood; they run away together.

ACT 4:
They get arrested.

ACT 5:
She (you're gonna love this) is sentenced to be deported to Louisiana, but she dies in des Grieux's arms.

COMPARE: Puccini's early opera Manon Lescaut (1893) is the Italian version of this melodic tear jerker. I'm glad I don't have to choose between them.

NORMA

VINCENZO BELLINI

BOTTOM LINE: A Druid priestess who has sacrificed her honor for the love of a Roman proconsul learns that he's fallen in love with a younger version.

ACT 1:

Druid high priest Oroveso tells his people that his daughter Norma (the high priestess) will signal them when it's time to revolt against the Roman occupiers. Unbeknownst to her people, Druid high priestess Norma has violated her oath of chastity and borne two children by Roman Proconsul (Military Governor) Pollione. And if that ain't bad enough, Pollione now has the hots for Adalgisa, a younger Druid priestess.

ACT 2:

Norma tries to kill her children but she can't. She summons her rival Adalgisa and, after one hell of a flashy duet, they become pals again. Norma heroically decides be burned to death for crimes against her people. Pollione, not to be outdone by a mere woman, chooses to die with her. (The resultant outpouring of melody is so eloquent that I'm damn near ready to walk into the fire with them.)

I PAGLIACCI
RUGGIERO LEONCAVALLO

BOTTOM LINE: A play-within-a-play within an opera: an actor finds out that his actress wife is fooling around ... so he kills her in both the Play and Real Life.

PROLOGUE:

Before the curtain goes up, Tonio the clown explains melodically that actors have feelings too, you know ...

ACT 1:

A troupe of actors arrive: Tonio, a hunchback clown, puts a move on actress Nedda, but he isn't her type, so she rejects him. But local boy Silvio _is_ her type: she agrees to meet him after the performance. Canio, her husband, overhears them. He is furious, heartbroken—but the play must go on—so he sings the most famous aria in opera: "Vesti la giubba..." "On with the greasepaint..."

ACT 2:

The Play: Nedda plays 'Columbine,' Beppe is 'Harlequin,' her back door man, Canio plays 'Pagliacco.' The play is a little too close to real life for the unstable Canio/Pagliacco, so he stabs his wife and her lover.

NOTE: There is a video of Pavarotti late in his career singing I _Pagliacci._ Luciano is no fool: he knew that the Voice, though still beautiful, is not what it once was-so for once in his life he decided to really act. And it was unbearable! Not because his acting was bad-because it was good. Too good. I saw a jealous maniac killing his wife. Honey, I don't know about you, but that isn't what I do opera for. Screw realism.

PETER GRIMES
BENJAMIN BRITTEN

BOTTOM LINE: Sad realism from England's top opera composer.

PROLOGUE:
In a little fishing village in England, fisherman Peter Grimes has lost an apprentice at sea in suspicious circumstances. He is acquitted at the inquest, but warned not to take another apprentice. Only Ellen the schoolmistress stands behind him.

ACT 1:
Balstrode, a retired sea captain, advises Grimes to leave the village and get a fresh start someplace else, but the stubborn Grimes says that he will force the town to respect him by becoming rich. Ellen arrives with a new apprentice for Grimes.

ACT 2:
Sunday, outside the church, Ellen sees bruises on the boy's neck and realizes that Grimes has abused the boy. She quarrels with Grimes, who hits her and storms off, taking the boy to his hut on the cliff top. The villagers take off after him. Grimes hears the mob coming, pushes the boy rudely, and the boy falls to his death. When villagers get to Grimes' hut, they see how neat and tidy it is, and decide that a guy that neat can't be so bad, so they go home.

ACT 3
Three days later, Grimes turns up at the village, exhausted. Balstrode tells him that the only way to redeem himself is to sail his boat out to sea and sink it. Grimes does.

PORGY & BESS
GEORGE GERSHWIN

BOTTOM LINE: White ids in black disguises.

ACT 1:

Crown, the local bully, kills a guy at a dice game and leaves town before the coppers can get him. His girlfriend Bess, a little too sexy to be invited in by any of the neighborhood ladies, has no place to live. Porgy, a cripple, lets her stay with him.

ACT 2:

Porgy and Bess are happy together. Bess sees Crown at a picnic. Crown, after months on the run, is most anxious to have a conversation of the flesh with Bess. Bess tries to resist but her spiritual side loses the battle to her hips. A storm overturns the boat of Jake (a fisherman). Crown and Jake's wife Clara go to help.

ACT 3:

Crown returns for Bess, and Porgy strangles him to death. While Porgy is in jail, Sportin' Life (a drug dealer) takes Bess to New York. Porgy, released from jail, follows them on his goat cart.

The Other Bottom Line: It's been a career-maker for some wonderful black singers and it provides jobs for others.

RIGOLETTO
GIUSEPPE VERDI

BOTTOM LINE: What goes around comes around.

ACT 1:

Count Monterone crashes the Duke of Mantua's party and denounces the dirty Duke for "deflowering" Monterone's innocent daughter. The Duke's hunchback jester, Rigoletto, makes cruel fun of old Monterone. The Duke has Monterone arrested, but before the coppers can take him away, Monterone puts a "father's curse" on the Duke and Rigoletto. Rigoletto, himself a father, turns away in terror.

ACT 2:

Duke, disguised as a student, visits Rig's daughter Gilda. The Duke's courtiers (royal groupies) think that Gilda is Rigoletto's mistress so, fun-loving guys that they are, they kidnap Gilda and take her to Duke.

ACT 3:

Rig begs for Gilda's release, but the Duke has deflowered her too.

ACT 4:

Rigoletto, profoundly pissed off, hires an assassin to ice the Duke. Gilda gets wind of the plan and sacrifices her own life for the dastardly Duke. When Rigoletto discovers that the body in the bag is his daughter, he screams, "*La Maledizione!*"—the friggin <u>curse</u>!

REAL Bottom Line: Easy to make fun of with some of the (justifiably) most famous music in opera. It isn't subtle, but for the most part, opera is not a subtle art form.

ROSENKAVALIER
RICHARD STRAUSS

An aging beauty gracefully surrenders her young lover to a girl his own age.

ACT 1:

The Marschallin, a 30-something married woman, realizes that her affair with Octavian, a 17-year-old boy (a "trouser role" sung by a woman) doesn't have much of a future. She sends him to deliver a silver rose (a token of engagement) to beautiful young Sophie ... on behalf of her fat old cousin Baron Ochs.

Strauss, to an extent that was unbelievable for a composer of his stature, wrote music that was almost exclusively for female singers. The most famous piece he wrote for a man is the tiny "Italian singer's aria" in Act 1 of *Rosenkavalier*. It is supposed to poke fun at Italian tenors, but it's gorgeous in spite of itself.

And nobody does it better than Pavarotti.

ACT 2:

Sophie falls in love with Octavian when he delivers the silver rose. She has never wanted to be with Baron Ochs, but her father insists ...

ACT 3:

Thanks to a neat bit of entrapment, Sophie's father sees what a womanizing oinker Baron Ochs is and Pops blesses Sophie's marriage to Octavian.

There is a famous movie of Rosenkavalier, starring Elisabeth Schwarzkopf. Personally, I couldn't help but notice (and notice and notice) the fact that Octavian–the boy–was a girl. That may work for some people, but I'm not one of them.

TALES OF HOFFMANN
JACQUES OFFENBACH

BOTTOM LINE: Drunken poet has the world's worst luck with women.

PROLOGUE:

Drunken poet Hoffmann tells everyone in the Tavern about the women he has loved—and lost.

ACT 1:

Hoffmann falls madly in love with Olympia. Unfortunately, she turns out to be a windup mechanical doll.

ACT 2:

Hoffmann falls madly in love with the courtesan Giulietta, a Venetian blonde. Unfortunately, she steals his shadow—his soul.

ACT 3:

Hoffman falls madly in love with Antonia, a singer. Unfortunately, she sings herself to death.

EPILOGUE:

Hoffmann, story finished, gets falling down drunk.

REAL Bottom Line: Despite serious flaws (e.g., musically and dramatically, Hoffmann is a spectator in his own story) Tales of Hoffmann (in this dude's opinion) is one of the finest half-dozen operas ever written.

TOSCA
GIACOMO PUCCINI

BOTTOM LINE: Love triangle in early 19th century Rome. The players: Cavaradossi (a painter), Tosca (a prima donna), Baron Scarpia (lecherous Chief of Police).

ACT 1:
Cavaradossi, painting a mural in church, pauses to hide Angelotti, an escaped political prisoner. Tosca, Cavaradossi's jealous girlfriend, drops by the church. So does Baron Scarpia.

The music that ends Act 1 (called the "Te Deum") is one of the coolest strokes in opera. Scarpia raves on in lip-smacking lust ("Ah, Tosca...") as the congregation prays and the nice church music plays in the background. (Puccini wasn't supposed to be that clever!)

ACT 2:
Scarpia has Cavaradossi thrown into prison and tortured. Tosca says she'll give herself to Scarpia if he lets Cavaradossi go free. Lecherous old Scarpia gives her two safe-conduct passes to escape Rome, but instead of keeping her end of the bargain, she stabs him.

ACT 3:
Cavaradossi, who according to plan, was to face a "fake" execution, finds to his great surprise, that the bullets are real. He dies. Despondent Tosca kills herself.

LA TRAVIATA
GUISEPPE VERDI

BOTTOM LINE: Courtesan finds true love, then has to reject innocent young bozo lover for his own good.

ACT 1:
Alfredo, a naïve young dude from the suburbs, meets Violetta (a Parisian courtesan), and they fall in love.

ACT 2:
The lovers live out in the country. Violetta peddles her jewelry to support them. Alfredo's father comes to Violetta to beg her to end the affair. (*He* says their relationship will prevent Alfredo's sister from marrying, but I'm not buying it!) Violetta relents and, without explaining to Alfredo, she moves back to Paris alone. Alfredo runs into her at a party and insults her and her escort. Alfredo's father arrives just in time to tell his son what a meathead he's been: *She did it for you, stupido!*

ACT 3:
Alfredo returns to Violetta. But she dies from consumption. (Personally, I think she croaks from singing too many razzle dazzle arias. The role is so brutal that a soprano who can sing the flashy coloratura in the first act is unlikely to have enough dramatic heft for the last act; and conversely, any sister hefty enough for the last act would probably be a klutz in the fancy-schmancy first act...

For What It's Worth: The Garbo movie *Camille* was based on the same play that the opera was taken from.

IL TROVATORE
GIUSEPPE VERDI

BOTTOM LINE: When you figure it out, you tell me.

ACT 1:

A Spanish lady (Leonora) loves Manrico, the "Troubadour." She throws herself into his arms but misses and ends up in the arms of Count di Luna, who also loves her. Manrico rushes off to sword fight with Mr. di Luna.

ACT 2:

An old gypsy broad named Azucena announces to her buddies that, unbeknownst to them, di Luna and Manrico are brothers. (Not *that* kind of brothers!) Leonora, having presumed that Manrico (a lover, not a fighter) was iced by di Luna, enlists in the convent. When Manrico learns that (1) Leonara is in a convent, and (2) his Prince is being attacked, he rushes off to (3) save his Prince from the bad guys and (4) save Leonara from the nuns.

Di Luna, waiting at the convent, sings such a beautiful aria *("Il Balen...")* that it's hard for us civilians to believe he's a bad guy. Manrico arrives at the last second and "spirits Leonara away."

ACT 3:

Azucena, Manrico's foster-mom, is captured. Manreek tries to rescue her but the inept fool is captured too.

ACT 4:

Leonora offers herself to di Luna if he'll free Manrico. Di Luna digs that, but Leonara outsmarts him(?) by poisoning herself. Di Luna kills Manrico, then learns (oy vey) that Manrico was his brother.

This is the opera that Groucho, Chico and Manrico Marx butchered in their totally insane movie, A Night at the Opera.

It's the kind of opera that doesn't lose a thing with the Marx Brothers' hijinks going on in the background!

THE
RING OF THE NIBELUNG
RICHARD WAGNER

OPERA 1
DAS RHEINGOLD
(PROLOGUE)

BOTTOM LINE: Wotan, chairman of the gods, has made so many shifty deals that they are starting to catch up with him.

SCENE 1:

Alberich, an ugly dwarf, steals gold guarded by the Rhine maidens, three young ladies who live under the Rhine River. (In Germany.)

SCENE 2:

Wotan and his nagging wife Fricka argue about the castle (Valhalla) being built for them by two giants. Fricka's sister, Freia, the goddess of youth, is to be traded for the castle—which means that the gods will get old. The giants say they'll accept the Rheingold, instead of Freia, IF they get it by that night.

SCENE 3 &4:

Wotan and Loge, the God of fire, trick Alberich and take the gold to pay for the castle.

OPERA 2
DIE WALKURE

BOTTOM LINE: The best and most melodic opera of the bunch.

ACT I:

Siegmund falls in love with Sieglinde (his sister), who is married to Hunding, who isn't too fond of visitors fondling his wife. So Sig and Sis run away.

ACT 2:

Fricka, the goddess of nagging wives, bitches out Wotan for whoring around (Siegmund is his illegitimate son) and disrespecting marriage. Wotan commands Brunnhilde (one of the nine warrior daughters of Wotan and Erda, the Earth Goddess) not to help the lovers, but Brunnhilde saves the pregnant Sieglinde. (Fricka really can't stand Brunnhilde because she's in-your-face proof of Wotan's whoring and she's Wotan's favorite daughter!)

ACT 3:

For disobeying him, Wotan puts Brunnhilde to sleep and surrounds her with fire so that only a fearless stud can save her.

(*That's* what happens; *this* is what it feels like: two people stand on a rock shouting for 20 minutes, then just as you're about to doze off, Wagner hits you with the most beautiful music imaginable ... the Music fills you with a sense of your own divinity, lifts you right out of your seat ...)

OPERA 3
SIEGFRIED

BOTTOM LINE: Siegfried the hero is even dumber than Manrico (the bubblehead from Il Trovatore).

ACT I

Siegfried, son of Siegmund and Sieglinde (Wagner was clearly from the George Foreman school of naming), is raised by a dwarf named Mime until the day he sings a big song about his magic sword.

ACT 2:

Siegfried kills a dragon and takes the dragon's magic ring.

ACT 3:

Siegfried finds Brunnhilde asleep on her fiery rock. When he awakens her, Brunnhilde, once a warrior goddess, is now a mortal woman in love with the dummy with a sword.

OPERA 4
GOTTERDAMMERUNG

BOTTOM LINE: *Gotterdammerung* (*Twilight of the Gods*) traces events leading to the end of the gods and their castle, Valhalla.

PROLOGUE:
The gods wait at Valhalla for the end. Siegfried marries Brunnhilde by giving her his magic ring. (He keeps his Batman Wristwatch for himself?)

ACT 1:
Hagen and Gunther (bad guys) plot to get the magic ring by giving Siggy a magic potion that will make him forget Brunnhilde and fall in lust with Gutrune (Gunther's sister). Sig, who is tough but not too bright, comes sailing down the Rhine right into their trap, drinks the magic potion, has a little guilt-free sex with Gutrune ("I swear, Brunnhilde, they drugged me.") Siegfried, who is no dumber without a memory than he was when he had one, goes up to bring back Brunnhilde and the Ring for Gunther.

ACT 2:
Siggy returns with Brunnhilde and the magic ring. She denounces everybody.

ACT 3:
Hagen kills Siegfried; Brunnhilde joins Siegfried on the burning funeral pyre and sings her glorious buns off, the Rhinegals get the magic ring, fire destroys the gods ... and well, that's about it.

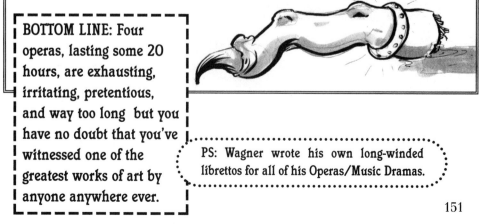

BOTTOM LINE: Four operas, lasting some 20 hours, are exhausting, irritating, pretentious, and way too long but you have no doubt that you've witnessed one of the greatest works of art by anyone anywhere ever.

PS: Wagner wrote his own long-winded librettos for all of his Operas/Music Dramas.

CURTAIN CALLS

The Scholarly Approach to Opera

I have poked a little fun at the scholarly approach to opera. I am now going to give you a pitch on behalf of it. Examining in detail all or part of an opera, or of opera in general; learning in-depth the difference between Opera Seria and Wagner's symphonic Music Dramas; studying composers or periods or libretti; or any of the other opera arcane I have teasingly called the intellectual approach to opera—when you reach the point when you want to examine any aspect of opera, **go for it**!

My intent here has been to engage your passion first and foremost, trusting that you will learn more about opera (or anything else) if you are driven by your own passion than if you approach it as if it were a list of facts. The scholarly approach is great when you're doing it from the heart.

Which brings us to Mr. Wagner's Ring Cycle. Nothing in opera rewards the intellectual approach more than Wagner's Ring. Go for it! I don't want you to follow me or anyone else. Get in touch with your own soul. Follow your own tastes.

BOTTOM LINE: use zealots and fanatics like Stefan Zucker, Wagner—and me—to broaden your arena of ecstasy, not to narrow it.

The Future of Opera—1

As the author of a book on opera, I should probably discuss modern opera, but if I do, I will infuriate opera directors. Truth: As a passionate listener, my ears say that opera croaked after Richard Strauss.

After the 1920s, creative composers took opera in directions that many listeners simply didn't love. *Wozzeck* (1925) and *Lulu* (written, 1935), by Alban Berg (1885-1935), were atonal operas that, depending upon your point of view, either enlarged the repertory or were forced down opera-lovers' throats. Leos Janacek (1854-1928), a Czechoslovakian composer, wrote several operas; the best—*Jenufa* (1903). *Peter Grimes* (1945) and *Billy Budd* (1951), by Britisher Benjamin Britten (1913-1976), are some people's cup of tea, and others not. Gian Carlo Menotti (1911-2007), an Italian who spent most of his life in America, is probably the most successful composer of "American" operas, including *Amahl and the Night Visitors* (1951) and *The Medium* (1946). The Ragtime opera *Treemonisha* (1915) by Scott Joplin (1868-1917) hasn't had much luck, whereas *Porgy and Bess* (1935) by George Gershwin (1898-1937) may have had more than it deserves. *Nixon in China*, by John Adams (1987), was a fair success.

Nobel Laureate Toni Morrison has written librettos for two operas, *Margaret Garner*, based on the main character in Morrison's majestic novel *Beloved* (2005—music by Richard Danielpour); and *Desdemona* (2011—music by Rokia Traore, Malian singer/songwriter). The pugnacious Morrison has written an opera in which Desdemona and the other women in Shakespeare's *Othello* "talk back" to Othello—and Shakespeare!

The Future of Opera—2

Truth? I don't believe the future of opera lies in any of the directions our opera houses are taking.

As I have made agonizingly clear, opera—for me and most opera fanatics—is an art based primarily on great opera **singers**. If you are new to opera, you can find treasures in opera's past. Singers from all over the world, going back 100 years; operas by our favorite composers ignored for no good reason. And blah, blah, blah ... *Don't give me the same old crap, Ron, baby. Give me something NEW!*

OK ... but don't come bitching at me if you don't like it.

I am going to offer a suggestion that is beyond "outside the box" ... so I need you to open your mind.

For people like me, the future of opera does NOT lie in the composing of new operas—**UNLESS** we could somehow resurrect Donizetti, Bellini, Wagner, Verdi and all the other composers we love?

We can! All we have to do is rewrite the operas we love so that the gender roles are reversed.

Lucia di Lammermoor becomes **LUIGI di Lammermoor**.

How about Bellini's **Norman**! (Maybe **Doris Godunov** is going a bit too far?)

Please believe me when I tell you that I am NOT joking here. I came up with the idea for this several years ago and wrote a novel about it. I imagined Pavarotti as the studly hero (the brain-dead Manrico) waiting in the wings as the music jiggled its way to the intro for Leonora's aria *"D'amor sull'ali rosee"* from Verdi's *Il Trovatore* ... and the heroic tenor gets so swept away by the beautiful song (he's heard it hundreds of times; he knows it by heart) that he begins singing the aria himself. The audience, transfixed by the glorious singing, can't help but love it. Thunderous applause when it's finished, then a sort of 'gender guilt' comes over everyone, singer and audience alike.

Superstud tenor's career is "diverted" (to say the least) with the result that he and a likeminded crew of singers create their own opera house and sing all the famous roles—gender reversed.

It would sell millions of CDs, DVDs, videos; it would sell out performances; most important of all, it would create some spectacular "new" music that was truly operatic, not some Greek hybrid wannabe called "musicdrama."

DISCOGRAPHY

Bellini	*Norma*	• (Intensely emotional) Callas, Ludwig, Corelli. Serafin-Angel
		• (Purely musical) Sutherland, Horne, Alexander, Cross. Bonynge-London
	I Puritani	• Callas, di Stefano, Panerai, Rossi-Lemini. Serafin-Angel
Bizet	*Carmen*	• Callas, Gedda. Pretre
		• (My hard-to-find favorite) Concita Supervia & Jose Luccioni (1930s)
Donizetti	*Elixir of Love*	• Either Pavarotti recording-with Joan Sutherland or Kathleen Battle
	Lucia di Lammermoor	• Callas, di Stefano, Gobbi. Serafin-Seraphim
Gounod	*Faust*	• Freni, Domingo, Allen, Ghiaurov. Pretre-London
Handel	*Rinaldo*	• Horne, Gasdia, Weidlinger, Palacio. Fisher-Nuova Era
Leoncavallo	*Pagliacci*	• It's a tenor's opera, so go with your favorite
Mascagni	*Cavalleria Rusticana*	• Callas, di Stefano,
		• Del Monaco, Suliotis
		• Bjoerling, Tebaldi
Massanet	*Manon*	• (French) Sills, Gedda, Souzay, Bacquier. Rudel-Angel
		• (Italian) Freni, Pavarotti, Panerai. Maaq-Verona
Mozart	*Abduction fr Seraglio*	• Auger, Grist, Schreier, Moll. Bohm-DG
	Don Giovanni	• Schwarzkopf, Welitsch, Gobbi, Dermota. Furtwangler-Olympic
		• Rethberg, Helletsgrube, Bokor, Borgioli, Pinza. Walter-Melodram
	Magic Flute	• Berger, Lemnitz, Belike, Roswaenge, Husch. Beecham-Nimbus (1938)
Mussorgsky	*Boris Godunov*	• Lear, Lanigan, Christoff. Cluytens-Angel
Offenbach	*Tales of Hoffmann*	• Either Placido Domingo (DG), Neil Shicoff (Angel) or Nicolai Gedda

Puccini	La Boheme	• Freni, Pavarotti, Panerai. Karajan-London
	Fanciulla del West	• Tebaldi, Del Monaco, MacNeil, Tozzi. Capuana-London
	Madame Butterfly	• Price, Tucker. Leinsdorf-RCA
	Manon Lescaut	• Albanese, Bjoerling, Merrill. Perlea-RCA Gold Seal
	Tosca	• Callas, di Stefano, Gobbi. De Sabata-EMI
Resphigi	La Fiamma (odd opera)	• Tokody, Takacs, Kelen, Solyom-Nagy. Gardelli-Hungaritone
Rossini	Barber of Seville	• Capsir, Borgioli, Stracciarai. Molajoli-Columbia (1929)
	L'Italiana in Algeri	• Horne, Battle, Palacio, Ramey, Zaccaria. Scimone-Erato
	Otello	• Von Stade, Carreras, Ramey. Lopez-Cobos-Philips
	Semiramide	• Studer, Larmore, Lopardo, Ramey. Marin-DG
Strauss	Guntram	• Tokody, Reiner Goldberg (fascinating tenor!), Solyom-Nagy. Queler-CBS
	Rosenkavalier	• Schwarzkopf, Stitch-Randall, Ludwig, Edelman. Karajan-
Verdi	Aida	• Price, Bumbry, Domingo, Milnes, Raimondi. Leinsdorf-RCA
		• Callas, Dominguez, Del Monaco. Defabritis-live, Mexico City (1951)
	Ernani	• Price (she'll kill you!), Bergonzi, Sereni. Schippers-RCA
	Rigoletto	• Callas, di Stefano, Gobbi. Serafin-EMI
	La Traviata	• Go with your favorite soprano-Callas, Albanese, Sills, Sutherland, Moffo
	Il Trovatore	• Plowright, Fassbender, Domingo, Zancanaro. Giulini-DG
Wagner	Parsifal	• Modl, Windgassen, London, Weber. Knappertsbusch-TelDec, 1951
	Mastersinger	• Janowitz, Fassbender, Konya, Unger, Stewart. Kubelik-NYTO 1969
	The Complete Ring Cycle: - Das Rheingold - Die Walkure - Siegfried - Gotterdammerung	• Modl, Konetzi, Jurinac,Grummer,Cavelti, Malaniuk, Klose, Suthaus, Windgassen, Patzak, Frantz, Frick. Neidlinger. Furtwangler-Angel

BIBLIOGRAPHY

BOOKS

Barber, David — WHEN THE FAT LADY SINGS. Toronto, Canada: Sound and Vision.

Blyth, Alan — OPERA ON CD. London: Kyle Kathy Ltd..

DiGaetani, John Lewis — AN INVITATION TO THE OPERA. New York: Anchor Books.

Ehrlich, Scott — PAUL ROBESON: ATHLETE, ACTOR, SINGER, ACTIVIST. Los Angeles: Melrose Sq. Publishing.

Englander, Roger — OPERA: WHAT'S ALL THE SCREAMING ABOUT? New York: Walker & Co.

Koestenbaum, Wayne — THE QUEEN'S THROAT. New York: Vintage Books.

Lebrecht, Norman — THE BOOK OF MUSICAL ANECDOTES. New York: The Free Press.

Lynch, Stacy Combs — CLASSICAL MUSIC FOR BEGINNERS. New York: Writers & Readers Pub.

Kolodin, Irving — THE OPERA OMNIBUS. Canada: Clark, Irwin & Co., Ltd.

McCourt, James — MAWRDEW CZGOWCHWZ. New York: The Noonday Press.

Mordden, Ethan — OPERA ANECDOTES. New York: Oxford University Press.

Pavarotti, Luciano — PAVAROTTI: MY OWN STORY. New York: Warner Books. (with William Wright)

Rice, Anne — CRY TO HEAVEN. New York: Pinnacle Books.

Rosenthal & Warrack — THE CONCISE OXFORD DICTIONARY OF OPERA. Oxford: Oxford •. Press.

Simon, Henry — 100 GREAT OPERAS AND THEIR STORIES. New York: Dolphin Books.

Stean, J.B. — VOICES: SINGERS & CRITICS. Portland, Oregon: Amadeus Press.

Stroff, Stephen — OPERA: AN INFORMAL GUIDE. Chicago: a capella books.

Walsh, Michael — WHO'S AFRAID OF CLASSICAL MUSIC? New York: Fireside Books.

Webster, James — Mozart's Operas and the Myth of Musical Unity.

RESOURCES

PERIODICALS & MAGAZINES

Opera News   The Metropolitan Opera Guild. New York.

Opera Quarterly   Duke University Press. Durham, North Carolina.

Opera Fanatic   The Magazine for Lovers of Expressive Singing. Bel
                    Canto Society. New York.

OTHER

SCHWANN Opus   Reference Guide to Classical Music. Santa Fe, New
                    Mexico.

Opera News
A publication of the Metropolitan Opera Guild
http://www.operanews.com/

The Opera Critic
The world's leading gateway and information resource for opera on the Internet
http://www.theoperacritic.com/
  Links to over 32,000 opera reviews in a range of languages
  Links to over 10,000 news-related items and articles on opera
  Links to CD and DVD reviews
  Schedule and casting information for over 300 opera companies around the world, including a dedicated page for each
  Over 20,000 production photos from around the world
  Dedicated pages for a range of featured singers, including Anna Netrebko, Renee Fleming, Thomas Hampson and many others
  A fully searchable database that allows you to access the extensive archives of The Opera Critic which go back over 10 years

News, reviews & headlines at The Opera Critic are updated daily. At-a-glance panels feature highlights of their ever-changing coverage.

San Diego Opera Podcasts
Contains news, live interviews, free Podcasts, reviews of current singers & performances, archives and other web sites pertaining to opera. NOT limited to San Diego. Podcasts feature 15-20 minute conversations with opera people from all over the world.
http://www.sdopera.com/Company/Education/Podcasts#view

Opera Now

"Provides a unique and all-encompassing perspective on the international opera scene through its lively and colourful mix of news, reviews, interviews, travel articles and commentary."
http://www.rhinegold.co.uk/magazines/opera_now/

Opera Today

Opera news, commentary, and reviews from around the world
http://www.operatoday.com/

San Francisco Opera

A great, super-informative web site for beginners & seasoned opera lovers alike.
http://sfopera.com/Learn/Opera-FAQs.aspx?gclid=CPyKz7XYiLICFSZxQ-godrmgA8Q

Opera Cast

A guide to opera broadcasts on the Internet, PLUS help for those of us who lack the skills to take full advantage of Internet radio & video broadcasts.
http://www.operacast.com/

Operanut.com

A list of one-click web sites that offer full operas or selections from opera.
http://www.operanut.com/radio.htm

Parterre Box – La Cieca

This web site is not for everybody ... but if you like it, you'll LOVE it!
http://parterre.com/

The Great Courses: Operas of Mozart

http://www.thegreatcourses.com/tgc/courses/course_detail.aspx?cid=780

The Bel Canto Society
Stefan Zucker

http://www.belcantosociety.org/pages/newsletter_signup.html
(WKCR-FM radio in NY)   http://en.wikipedia.org/wiki/NewYorkCity
http://www.operafanatic.com/info/stefan-zucker
http://www.belcantosociety.org/store/product_info.php?products_id=491

Metropolitan Opera Saturday
Afternoon Opera Broadcasts

Metropolitan Opera High Definition
Theater Videocasts

SOME GREAT YOUTUBE SELECTIONS

Whitney Houston's 1991 singing of "The Star-Spangled Banner" is considered by many (myself included) to be the best version of the U.S. national anthem ever recorded. It became a top-ten best seller (twice) and was among Houston's best selling recordings.
http://www.youtube.com/watch?v=drDSALCKH_Y'

Pavarotti – The Italian Singer's Aria ("Di rigore armato il seno" from Strauss' *Der Rosenkavalier*
http://www.youtube.com/watch?v=M-UQt5HXWnQ&feature=related

Bjorling & Tebaldi – "O soave fanciulla..." Puccini's *La Boheme*
http://www.youtube.com/watch?v=yn7bQXnIx_k&feature=related

Jessye Norman – Dido's Lament – "When I am laid in earth..." Purcell's *Dido & Aeneas*
http://www.youtube.com/watch?v=jOIAi2XwuWo

Janet Baker –- Dido's Lament – "When I am laid in earth..." Purcell's *Dido & Aeneas*
http://www.youtube.com/watch?v=D_50zj7J50U

Jeff Buckley – Dido's Lament – "When I am laid in earth..." Purcell's *Dido & Aeneas*
http://www.youtube.com/watch?v=CqYw7mtYOxE&feature=related

The Shawshank Redemption – Mozart – "Sull'aria" from "The Marriage of Figaro" sung by Gundula Janowitz and Edith Mathis
http://www.youtube.com/watch?v=Bjqmg_7J53s

Anna Moffo – "D'amor sull'ali rosee" from Verdi's *Il Trovatore*
http://www.youtube.com/watch?v=42j-Tgp-Vyw&feature=related

Billie Holiday – "I'm a fool to want you ..."
http://www.youtube.com/watch?v=Xs9P-pfqF6Y

Maria Callas – "Qui la voce sua soave" from Bellini's *I Puritani*
http://www.youtube.com/watch?v=hGtnHjcIH4M

Billie Holiday – "Gloomy Sunday"
http://www.youtube.com/watch?v=x8dNSiN3jhE

Maria Callas – "Suicidio!" from Ponchielli's *La Gioconda*
http://www.youtube.com/watch?v=hAXJ8pAQUns&feature=related

Kiri Te Kanawa – Marietta's Lied – Korngold – *Die Tote Stadt*
http://www.youtube.com/watch?v=XIIk6A72VQI

Caruso – Journet – Aida
http://www.youtube.com/watch?v=z_s7WtV5ERo&feature=related

Rethberg – Gigli – Pinza – "Qual volutta transcorrere" – Verdi's *I Lombardi*
http://www.youtube.com/watch?v=n8COF03w0KY

Gigli – Nadir's aria – Bizet's *Pearlfishers*
http://www.youtube.com/watch?v=Pn5XnM5Fg9E

Smokey Robinson – "Ooh baby baby..."
http://www.youtube.com/watch?v=5RDUYOSpH9w

Aretha Franklin – "Nessun dorma"
http://www.youtube.com/watch?v=GmXkEhs00lo

Mahalia Jackson – "Abide with Me"
http://www.youtube.com/watch?v=cZ5uHVxsWG4

Jussi Bjorling – "Amor ti vieta..." from *Fedora* by Giordano
http://www.youtube.com/watch?v=sC2NTbm4AEs

Andrea Bocelli – Il mare calmo della sera
http://www.youtube.com/watch?v=Pj3IIvrNWBY

Did You Know, Yo...?

Popular singers often record Opera arias:

- **Della Reese**'s hit, **"Don't You Know"** is Musetta's Waltz from **Puccini's** *La Boheme*
  http://www.youtube.com/watch?v=VJSnKWpb_hs
- **Jackie Wilson**'s big recording of "**Night**" is Delilah's aria from **Saint-Saens'** *Samson and Delilah*
  http://www.youtube.com/watch?v=sXitw5_7Wzs&feature=related
  (It's terrible! R&B Gigli!)
- 50s crooner Tony Martin sings Prologue from Pagliacci -
  http://www.youtube.com/watch?v=77IN4Fb8StI
- Tony Williams – The Platters – "My Prayer" -
  http://www.youtube.com/watch?v=FTqoTZ3IPsA

(Worth hearing.)

The "For Beginners" web site— and the 'Google-&-YouTube' combo

The "For Beginners" web site will have a page with the one-click URLs that will take you directly to the **YouTube** selections listed above, and many others. The Music-on-YouTube page will be updated regularly ... but remember: You can find any piece of music you like by using the **Google-&-YouTube** combination.

The Internet is now so "generous" that, between Google & YouTube, you have instant access to the most current operas, singers, performances, etc.

APPENDIX

Shawshank & The Fat Lady Revisited

Q: Some intros to opera begin, "Now that you have a ticket to a live opera performance ...?"

A: An introduction to opera should not assume you already have a ticket to the opera—that's leaving the most difficult part undone.

I have tried to entice you to buy that ticket.

Q: Some introductions to opera suggest that people are already aware of opera's power to arouse great passions and inspire "outpourings of unadulterated ecstasy." How do you feel about that?

A: I think that's putting the cart before the horse. If people had the slightest notion they stood a good chance of experiencing *outpourings of unadulterated ecstasy* from listening to opera, they'd be a lot more eager to get to it. I have never seen an intro to opera that explained <u>how</u> one goes about experiencing these emotional outpourings of unadulterated ecstasy? They don't even *ask* the question, let alone try to answer it.

I have tried to answer that question.

Q: How does one go about choosing opera singers?

A: Sample as many singers as you can in whichever formats you prefer: CDs, DVDs, YouTube, radio, TV, live concerts, live operas, Met Opera Radio or TV broadcasts, Met Opera High Definition Theater Videocasts, free radio opera performances from all over the world—snoop the dozens of web sites that feature opera (see **Resources** section); listen and/or watch as many different opera singers as you can ... *and pay attention to what gives you pleasure.*

This book aims to be a pleasure-driven introduction to opera!

Q: Do you have to go to the opera house to begin listening to opera.

A: No. You begin listening at home, looking for a voice or two that pushes your buttons. Like every opera nut I know, I have had some of my most intense experiences listening from home or in the course of my everyday life.

Q: Give us an example.

A: A few years ago, training for a marathon race, I scheduled my long runs for Saturday afternoons so I could listen to Met Opera broadcasts. This day featured Placido Domingo singing *Otello*. Running through one of the ugliest places on earth (from Hoboken, NJ, through the tangle of roads to and from the Lincoln Tunnel toward Weehawken—UGLY!) ... Domingo starts singing his heart out (**Dio**! **Mi potevi**...) ... I'm running, tears all down my face, impervious to cars lane-hopping, horns honking, drivers cursing, breathing exhaust fumes instead of air, lifted high above the ugliness, but forcing myself to be careful because Domingo's singing is making me feel bullet-proof.

(I was so filled with the power of the music that I felt that any car that hit me would just bounce off me!) And Otello's death scene (**Niun mi tema**...)—forget about it! Like the dude in *Chariots of Fire*, I felt God's pleasure. That feeling, whatever you call it, is one of the pleasures I get from opera.

And you don't have to go to the opera house to get it!

Q: Does this book aim to do anything we might not be aware of?
A: Yes. (Or maybe.) I have tried to use *The Shawshank Redemption* to emphasize the fact that the power of music you don't quite understand to move you beyond your limits can be intensely liberating if you trust it and let it work its magic. If you let it happen, the payoff can be glorious.

Best case: You get a taste of transcendent ecstasy! (Or not.)

Q: Opera books are very specific about which operas to see but they don't seem to be the least bit fussy about the singers.
A: Professional critics and musicians generally consider opera singers a necessary evil—gifted morons who contribute nothing of real artistic value to opera. They will rave about composers and conductors—but not SINGERS! Most opera reviews have more to say about the "production" (the crap on the stage) than about the singers.

A Few Things Worth Mentioning

- **Sub-Titles & Super-titles**: Virtually all operas nowadays give you the translated text of what the characters are saying (singing). Sub-titles (text at the bottom of the screen) are usually used in videos and DVDs. Super-titles (text at the top of the screen) are usually used in the opera house.

- **Does It Matter Where You Are Seated in the Opera House?** YES, of course it does. Books and articles that are eager to get you into the opera house downplay the importance of where you are seated, but the difference can be enormous. The closer the better.

- **Dress** any way you like ... but don't applaud until you hear other people applaud. Just about the only way to make a fool of yourself at a live opera is applauding at the wrong time.

A Special Thanks to Stefan Zucker

Stefan Zucker (b. 1949) is an American opera singer, an expert in Italian opera and the profoundly eccentric editor of **Opera Fanatic** magazine and former host of the radio program of the same name.

Zucker wrote, edited, published, organized, broadcast, ate, slept and dreamed about *Opera Fanatic* magazine and radio show. He knows and loves singing as much as any fanatic on earth. Although he is obsessively devoted to singers like **Magda Olivero,** he encouraged different opinions and he treated everyone who phoned into his radio show with respect.

> **Dear Stefan, you taught me more about singing than anyone in the world. You gave me a taste of operas and singers I had never heard before. I've never met you, I just wanted to thank you.**
>
> —Ron David.

Snoop through opera's past. It's a goldmine of spectacular singers. Zucker even puts out an Opera Fanatic's Catalogue, featuring hard-to-get videos, tapes, CDs.

Zucker's New York area radio show was the best program I've ever heard for learning about opera, especially about singing. In addition to guests like Franco Corelli and Carlo Bergonzi, a constant parade of true opera fanatics and connoisseurs phoned in with commentary that ranged from brilliant to outrageous. Zucker's show was a cross between an encyclopedia of singing and the *National Enquirer.*

Q: How is it Possible for the Sound Quality of Old Recordings to Improve?
A: A perfect example of not only how the sound quality can be improved dramatically, but of how much work and dedication it takes can be seen in the first half of this *NY Times* article:

Beyond High C, High Technology
by William G. Honan in *The New York Times*

For the love of opera, Stefan Zucker trained to reach the upper limits of the tenor's range.

For the love of opera, Stefan Zucker spent 12 years of Saturday nights as the host of "Opera Fanatic," a radio show on WKCR-FM that featured rare recordings, interviews with performers and call-ins. ⟶

And for the love of opera, Stefan Zucker has reinvented himself as a techno geek.

Mr. Zucker, 55, has learned that the computer can be his friend. After Columbia University, the owner of WKCR-FM, dropped Mr. Zucker as the host of 'Opera Fanatic' in 1994, he turned his efforts to preserving early opera recordings and films through his nonprofit Bel Canto Society. There, at www.belcantosociety.org, fellow fanatics can hear his old radio programs and purchase his remastered CD's, DVD's and videos.

As a result, Mr. Zucker—cheerful and shaggy-bearded—says that when he is not listening to music, he likes nothing more than to curl up with a current issue of the Journal of the Audio Engineering Society.

"I started as a singer," Mr. Zucker said, " and soon became fascinated by the way in which singing had evolved."

Recently, Mr. Zucker acquired for Bel Canto Society a live recording of a 1939 "Il Trovatore" performance starring Jussi Bjorling and Gina Cigna. The original was made on a 78 r.p.m. recording marred by fluctuations in speed and audible clicks and pops.

Mr. Zucker said that it could take as much as three hours on a digital audio work station to delete just one of the 900-odd clicks or pops on the original without compromising the music. He also adjusted playback speed in 10th-and 20th-of-a-percent increments, making more than 500 corrections. "If you don't get the speed right," he explained, "not only is the sound off pitch but it is also off in timbre, or sonority." The remastering took five months.

"It took that long," he said, "because you have to isolate the sounds you don't want and then suppress them, and maybe restore some if you think you've gone too far. It's a very delicate process. Bel Canto Society sells the two-disk CD set for $19.95, so you can see this isn't a get-rich-quick scheme."

He goes to similar lengths for his film restorations. To restore "Carnegie Hall," a 1947 film that includes performances in the hall by Jan Peerce, Fritz Reiner, Risë Stevens, Ezio Pinza, Bruno Walter, Lily Pons and a dozen others, Mr. Zucker struck a deal with a British collector who had a 35-millimeter print and wanted to trade it for a number of videos. Then Mr. Zucker kept searching for additional prints, eventually splicing together bits and pieces from 13 separate prints.

Why go to so much trouble? "Well," Mr. Zucker said, "when people watch and listen to the finished product, I see them leap with joy.

"I'm also motivated by the fact that I'm in a race against time. I'm trying to preserve these films before they disintegrate and before the collectors die and the films get discarded."

(See the rest of the article at http://www.enotes.com/topic/Stefan_Zucker)

As wonderful and unique as Stefan Zucker's passion for opera is, his voice ... well, remember that screechy-voiced guy named Tiny Tim—that's what Zucker's voice sounds like to me.

THE FOR BEGINNERS® SERIES

www.forbeginnersbooks.com